NEW HOME SALE$

Start today building your secure future!

Diane Taylor

NEW HOME SALE$

THE HOW-TO BOOK FOR A HIGH INCOME CAREER!

New Home Sales Leader

DIANE TAYLOR

BROWN BOOKS PUBLISHING GROUP
DALLAS, TEXAS

For information, please contact
Brown Books Publishing Group
16200 North Dallas Parkway, Suite 170
Dallas, Texas 75248
972.381.0009
www.BrownBooks.com

First Printing, 2003

ISBN 0-9740121-0-6
LCCN 2003093849
Printed and bound in the United States of America

For Al

"To the world you might be one person,
but to one person you might be the world."

—Unknown

CONTENTS

ACKNOWLEDGMENTS

There were times during the writing of this book that I behaved like a spoiled child. I preferred to be totally alone and was selfishly self-absorbed in my toy—writing. I must apologize to and thank those who loved and encouraged me. Without these wonderful people, this book would not have been possible.

Al Taylor, my husband who believes I can do anything! The secret is, when I am with him, the whole world is magical even me. Mama and Joyce for letting me call and whine.

My grandsons, Joshua and Cotton Rasco, whose chocolate chip kisses and little boy hugs kept me going. Thanks to my daughter, Heather, for all those wonderful Thursdays. Don Harbour and Jeremy Larsen, my dream team architects. Michele Cox, my dear friend and the best speller in Texas. Thanks to the Garden Club for sharing my dream and sowing seeds of encouragement. Thanks to my niece Jobeth Andreacchio for reading the rough draft and encouraging me to finish. Kathryn Grant, the best editor any writer could hope for. Alyson Alexander, whose creative mind turns mediocre into fabulous. Eddie Bearden for his insightful editing. A special thanks to my publisher, Milli Brown, for her vast knowledge, experience, and wise guidance.

INTRODUCTION

A career in new home sales can be one of the most exciting and rewarding available today. Six-figure incomes are common to those who are well trained. But without proper training, new home sales can also be an adventure into no money, customers canceling contracts, and daily arguments between sales and construction. The nice thing is it does not have to be that way. The goal of this book is to help a person, even on the first day as a new home sales consultant, to have the knowledge and confidence needed to get the sale. This book also works as a great refresher course for the experienced sales consultant. If you find your sales are lagging, pull out this book and go back to the basics.

Successful new home sales consultants need to acquire a working knowledge of mortgage finance, construction, blueprints, and plot plans. They also need to learn how to overcome buyers' objections. It is important to develop excellent follow-up skills and learn how to put deals together.

My first year in the new homes sales industry I made a mere $10,000. All around me, experienced sales consultants were making ten times that. I quickly realized the difference between the successful consultants and myself was not personality, clothes, or fancy cars, but *knowledge*.

The successful sales consultants had acquired the moneymaking mechanics of this industry through years of working on-site. I did not want to wait years for the big bucks! I needed to get the facts quickly and start cashing in on a great career!

I read everything I could get my hands on, but everything seemed to be written for people who already understood the basics. I needed someone to take me by the hand and say in simple words, "This is how it works." Unfortunately, I never found that person or that book. So . . . I went back to school and took every class offered on mortgage banking, loan origination, loan processing, loan underwriting, and loan servicing. I talked to mortgage bankers. I bugged my on-site construction manager with a zillion questions about the building process. I talked to architects. I talked to successful new home sales consultants. There is no short cut to success. It takes time, hard work, and a willingness to learn. As I acquired the knowledge, the money followed. It will be the same for you.

After reading and studying this book you will not know everything about the housing industry. You will remove self-doubt caused by a lack of knowledge. The basics are laid out in easy-to-understand words. If you commit to learn and practice what is written in the following pages, you will acquire the confidence needed to guide a prospective buyer through the process. Your knowledge will build trust with your prospects and buyers.

People buy from people they like and, most of all, trust.

Make a commitment to change your life. Use this book as a guide to become the best.

Diane Taylor

CHAPTER 1

HOW TO GET STARTED

The first step in preparing for a career in new home sales is to contact the real estate commission in your state and ask if a real estate license is a requirement for selling new homes. A list of the regulatory agencies in the United States and the Canadian provinces and territories is included in this book.

If you have never worked in the new home sales industry, phone your local Home Builders Association (HBA) for a listing of all the builders in your city. If there is not an HBA in your immediate vicinity, contact the National Association of Home Builders (NAHB) at 800-368-5242 to obtain information on state or local Home Builders Associations. The mailing address for the NAHB is:

National Association of Home Builders
1201 15th Street, NW
Washington, DC 20005-2800

Another good source to obtain information on area builders is your local newspaper. The Saturday and Sunday editions in larger cities offer a section on new homes. The builders run ads in this section and list the locations of their communities, the price ranges of each community, and any discount or promotion they are offering for the weekend or the month.

Once you have compiled a list of the builders in your area, you will need to research each builder for the type of construction they offer. There are generally two classifications for builders: custom builders and production builders.

Custom builders rarely hire rookies, and the cost of custom homes tends to be higher than production homes. Custom builders work directly with a client to create a client's mental vision of a house and turn the vision into reality. The client is involved with each step of the blueprinting and product selection processes. Changes are made daily if requested by the client. The cost of creating a custom home is estimated at time of contract. The actual finished price tends to run higher than the estimate.

Production builders vary greatly in price ranges offered to the public. A production builder will purchase sets of blueprints from architectural firms. The builder seldom allows buyers to make changes to the prints. A buyer is given the full purchase price at contract subject only to the buyer adding a few upgraded products such as a better grade of carpet or light fixtures.

Production builders often offer training classes for novices. Custom builders hire experienced, well-trained sales consultants. You will need to assess yourself. What price ranges are you best suited to sell? Do you need training? Can you sell custom? Do you have the skills necessary to sell first time homebuyers? Are you able to work from blueprints to sell the custom buyer?

A first-time homebuyer, buying a production home, is different from a custom buyer. A first-time homebuyer may need help in understanding mortgages and the entire construction process. A custom buyer is more savvy. This buyer usually has owned or built several homes and has a working knowledge of mortgages and the building process. The custom buyer can be more demanding than a first-time home-buyer and will expect more from his on-site salesperson. A custom sales counselor must be able to meet with the architect and discuss changes. The sales counselor will be part of each stage of the building process and will report daily to the buyer, the trades, and the builder. Custom sales counselors are responsible for tracking expenses as the project progresses.

After deciding your selling niche based on your abilities, put a brief resume together. If you do not have any experience in new home sales, I suggest a cover letter. Sell yourself hard in this letter. Keep the contents brief and create a "kick paragraph" in the cover letter. Here are a few suggestions for kick paragraphs.

A. I understand sales as an industry, and I possess the ability to present a product and close quickly. May I present myself to you?

B. My goal is to become a top producer selling custom homes. I feel with your leadership and my desire, I could make a difference in ABC Builders' bottom line.

C. I have a good working knowledge of the mortgage and con-struction industry. I can make the purchasing process easy to understand. I work well with first time buyers as well as the experienced buyer. I could make your job less stressful!

Your local library is an excellent source for examples of resumes and how to create a cover letter. Keep your resume to one page and be truthful. A straightforward, clean-looking format is essential.

When applying for a job with a builder, do not state in your resume that you are seeking a full and/or a part time position. Be decisive.

Do you want to work as a full time sales counselor? Do not put on your resumé applying for either an assistant or a sales counselor position. You cannot be both. You are either qualified to be an assistant or you are a qualified salesperson. Applying for two positions in one resume is never a good idea.

Call the corporate office of all the building companies you are interested in applying to for a sales position and ask for the requirements for their sales counselors. Also ask if they offer training. Get the name and fax number for the sales manager. Large companies can have two, three, or four sales managers covering different areas or divisions. You need contact information for all of them and to send a resume to each sales manager. A manager of one division may not be looking to add sales-people and could file your resume, while the manager in another division of the same company could need someone immediately.

Place your resumes in large envelopes addressed to the individual sales managers and, if possible, hand deliver the envelopes to the corporate office.

If you hand deliver your resume, always ask the receptionist if there is a sales manager available to speak with you. Dress as though you were going to an interview. Make a good impression on anyone who sees you. A sales manager could walk into the lobby while you are dropping off your resume. Would he or she want to talk to someone in jeans and a t-shirt? Professionals always look professional in a work environment. Be prepared to meet your future.

Do not despair if you do not get the impromptu interview. Remember in sales we *ask* for everything! Sometimes we get it, and sometimes we don't.

After delivering your resume, wait two days and call the manager or managers to inquire if they have received and had a chance to review your resume.

Be persistent. Show your follow-up skills. When you get turned down for a position, call the sales manager back and ask if he or she would be willing to tell you why they were unable to use you as a salesperson. Could they give you some pointers that could help you in your next interview?

Ask them to be direct. You cannot become a top producer if you are unaware of the areas in which you need improvement. Tell them you would appreciate their advice. If the reason is lack of experience, ask the manager if he/she could suggest a company that hires people with a burning desire to get into the industry, like you! Be passionate, you are selling! If they offer the name of a company, quickly ask if they can give you a contact person. If they give you a name, ask if you may tell this person you received their name from him/her? Thank them and hang up.

GOOD MANNERS MAKE GOOD IMPRESSIONS

After you contact the other company and sales manager, send a note in the mail to the manager who gave you the lead. In the note, thank them again for taking the time to talk with you and express your appreciation for the lead for XYZ builders. In your note, say if it worked out or not. If it did not create a job for you, state that it did not work out, but you are not discouraged and will keep trying. Sign your note and include your phone number.

When you do get a job, send notes to everyone who interviewed you. In this card, thank the person for seeing you and state that you hope to see them again one day. Keep a list of these managers.

If your area has a Sales and Marketing Council, get a schedule of the council meetings held by your local HBA. The Sales and Marketing Council is an organization made up of builders, sales counselors, developers, title companies, mortgage companies, and anyone associated with the homebuilding process. When you attend the meetings, make it a point to re-introduce yourself to all the managers who interviewed you. It is a great place to get your name and face before the homebuilding world.

OTHER WAYS TO ENTER NEW HOME SALES

Are you willing to begin as a sales assistant? Many companies are not willing to hand over a multi-million dollar community to a newcomer and will require beginners to work under an experienced salesperson for six months to a year.

An assistant's job includes the following:
- All clerical duties and maintaining the buyers' files
- Locking and unlocking the spec houses
- Inspect the models on a daily basis to insure they are immaculate
- Schedule the cleaning of the models and spec houses
- Daily walk through every house under construction and report the status of each house to the sales counselor
- Report on the overall curb appeal of the neighborhood
- Meet and greet each and every person who enters the model
- Attempt to get a guest card from each visitor
- Works for the sales counselor
- Free the sales counselor from any duties other than selling

In an assistant training program, the assistant is usually paid hourly and may or may not be compensated for sales they procure. Any assistant bonus will in most instances come out of the commission of the sales counselor who is training the assistant. The sales counselor is not always required to give a bonus to an assistant.

When interviewing for an assistant program, ask about compensation for your sales or bonus programs and get a specific time period for your apprenticeship before signing on.

In the beginning of my career, to gain experience I worked several weekends for a sales counselor without pay. I turned these free weekends into major training sessions. I gained on-site selling experience and improved my negotiating skills. You must be willing to give 100% of yourself to learn this business.

The best resource for getting into new home sales is on-site sales counselors. New home sales counselors are always networking. If you know someone working in the industry as a sales counselor, ask if they would be willing to help you get an interview with their builder. If their company is not hiring, ask if they know of a builder who is hiring. Ask how they got started.

If you do not know any sales counselors, get in your car, go on-site, and meet some! Just pop into a sales office. If they are busy, go to the next location on your list. Just a small tip here: on-site sales counselors get asked daily, or rather told daily, "Gee, I think I could do what you do." Top producers have worked hard on their craft to make it appear simple. Do not start your conversation with that silly sentence. Begin with a good introduction of yourself and tell the sales counselor you have been applying for sales positions. Ask if they would like to have some free help on a weekend.

Do not take up a lot of their time. A top producer works with an appointment book. Do not call and ask for an appointment to talk to them about getting into sales. Their appointment book is for planning productive days. They schedule appointments to sell houses. If you get lucky and meet a sales counselor that is willing to share information with you, be gracious and brief. You should use the same note card follow-up you used with the sales managers.

Getting started in new home sales takes perseverance and persistence. If you want it, it is up to you to make it happen!

CHAPTER 2

MONEY

How are sales counselors compensated? How much money can you make? Not all building companies have the same compensation program. You need to ask about their payment plan in your interview. Following are compensation scenarios I compiled from interviewing sales managers from ten production building companies located in Dallas, Texas.

COMPANY ONE

New hires are offered one or two months' salary of $2,500. Beginning the third month the sales counselor is on commission only. The commission is 2% of the final sales price of the home, excluding swimming pools. Builders cannot pay a salesperson on an item they do not make any money on. The commission is paid when the house closes. Ask about their build time. If a builder has slow construction it will affect your income.

COMPANY TWO

The new hire's first month's salary is negotiated with the sales manager when the position is offered to the sales counselor. The length of time for the salary (one month or longer) is negotiated. If a sales counselor is going into a trailer or a community without completed or near completed spec/inventory homes, it will be important to negotiate a longer salary period. The commission rate is 2% on build jobs, and 2% on a spec if it is sold before completion. After completion of a spec house, the commission rate is adjusted up or down.

COMPANY THREE

No salary is available and the commission is graduated. The first sale, the commission is 1.5%. The second sale of the month, the commission increases to 1.75% of the sales price of the home. The third sale of the month and any others in that month will be paid 2% of the sales price of the home. The process begins all over again the next month. Payment is made the month after the house closes.

COMPANY FOUR

All sales counselors are on a monthly draw of $3,500. They are paid commissions of 2% less their draw. Commissions are paid after the houses close. There is not a beginning salary. The commission rate is based on experience. This means you could negotiate a higher commission rate coming into the company. The company offers to increase a sales counselor's base commission rate at annual reviews based on performance. If a sales counselor excelled and was awarded 2.5% for the upcoming year, or even 3%, this commission rate is only for the time period specified. The following year, the sales manager will review the sales counselor's production, and the commission rate could revert to 2%. The highest commission available for a sales counselor is 3%.

COMPANY FIVE

No beginning salary and no draw: sales counselors are paid 2% of the company's sales price of the house excluding items sold at the company design center. After the sales counselor writes the contract, collects $5,000 earnest money from the buyer, and the buyer has provided a pre-qualification letter, the salesperson may collect half of their commission or 1%. The remaining 1% is paid the month after the house closes. I have worked with this pay structure and never went without a paycheck. The earnest money was collected at time of the contract and the loan letter was obtained within seven days of the date of the contract. If a buyer cancels, any monies the company has paid to you will be deducted from your next check.

COMPANY SIX

The company offers one month's salary. The amount is negotiable. There is no draw. The commission rate is 2% for all sales counselors. Sales counselors are paid in thirds. One-third of the commission paid at time of contract, another third after loan preapproval and completion of the red line meeting. The final third of the commission is paid the first month after the house closes. I worked this scenario and found the bookkeeping to be maddening.

COMPANY SEVEN

The company pays a draw of $5,000, 2% commission, and never pays commission payments until the first month after the houses close. There is no beginning salary, and the company will not offer you any compensation for money you may have left on the books at another company to come join this one. This is a key point. If you are in the business and decide to go with another company for whatever reason, try to negotiate a portion of the monies you are leaving. This will usually be paid to you in a longer salary period. In this situation you could be collecting salary as well as commissions from your closings if you jump in and sell some specs.

COMPANY EIGHT

A new company has arrived on the scene in Dallas, Texas, and is offering 2.5% commission to experienced sales counselors. A draw of $5,000 per month is optional. Sales counselors are paid on the final numbers listed on the buyer's HUD closing statement. This means if your buyer goes to the company design center and purchases an additional $10,000/$50,000/$100,000 in options and upgrades, you will be paid on these items. Remember some companies pay sales counselors on structural items only. A structural item would be an optional media room, optional game room, optional extra bedrooms, and baths. Design center options would include upgraded carpet, countertops, hardwood floors, and window blinds just to name a few. Not getting paid on design center options can put a dent in your income.

COMPANY NINE

Two month's salary is offered. The amount is negotiated. There is a mandatory draw of $3,500 per month and the draw cannot be increased. Sales counselors are paid 2% with the opportunity to increase the commission rate based on performance. After the sales counselors have sold $6,000,000, their commission rate is increased to 2.5% for the remainder of the year. Commissions are paid after the houses close.

COMPANY TEN

A draw of $2,500 is available but not mandatory. Sales counselors are paid .8% on the first sale. One percent commission is paid on the second sale, with 1.5% commission on the third sale, and 2% on the fourth and all other sales in the month. Each month the sales counselors begin at .8% again. This company hires rookies, and they offer an excellent training program. The company also has one of the highest sales counselors' turnovers in the industry. The company has all 2-person offices. With a partner it will be difficult for you to consistently make four sales a month.

As you can see there are many different compensation programs. Your interview is the time to talk about money. The key word is to negotiate what will work for you and your family. How much are you worth? What are you bringing to the table? Ask if the company has a benefit program. All the companies in the ten scenarios offered medical benefits and 401(k) programs. The 401(k) programs differed slightly as to the company match, vested time, and how soon before a new hire would be eligible to join. You should look at the company as hard as they are looking at you.

HOW MUCH MONEY CAN YOU MAKE?

There is no limit to your ability to earn a huge income. However, be smart. If you are offered a job in a neighborhood with a history of one sale per month, you cannot expect a 6-figure income. You need to research the area. Are the schools good or bad? What are the negatives of the surrounding area and the community you will be selling? What is the build time for the community? How many lots are in the com-munity? How many specs? How many specs does the builder like to keep on the ground in a community—4, 10, or none? Will you have one part-ner or two? Does the company have one-person offices? Do they pay for assistants? How many hours will they pay for an assistant, 16 hours (your days off), or is the assistant full-time with benefits? Can you choose your days off? Can you take 2 consecutive days off together? Do you have to take split days? Are the sales offices open on all holidays? Are religious and federal holidays observed?

There are so many questions you need to ask during the interview. Any one of the above questions could affect your income potential and your family life. Do not be afraid to ask these questions. Asking questions will not keep you from getting the job. It will ensure a good match between you and the company.

When called for an interview ask the sales manager if he will tell you the area and community he wants to interview you for, and say that you would like to drive the community before you two get together to talk. Do not go into the sales office and quiz the on-site salesperson you will be replacing. You do not know the reason behind his or her leaving. If you want to see the model home go on the salesperson's day off. The sales manager will give you this information. Before interviewing or accepting a position, you should shop the competition in the community. Have sales been good? You can tell if the community is not selling just by driving through and counting the number of homes under construction. How long has the community been open? How many sales were in the community last month? If it is an established community, how many sales and closings did the company have last year?

Always ask the sales manager why the current salesperson is leaving the community. Was the salesperson fired or transferred to another com-munity? If they were fired, ask in your interview why they were fired. If they were fired for lack of sales, was this because there is a problem with the community, or was the sales counselor not suited for that price range? You will know before the interview by checking out the community if the problem is area related. You need to hear from the sales manager why they are making a change in personnel.

Is this community a closeout? A closeout community is one in the final stages of construction and sales. A closeout community can have one to fifteen houses left to sell. Ask what your options will be with the company after you close out the community. Do not be afraid to take a closeout community. Closeouts usually have all specs, and this can mean instant money. If this is not a close out and the community has shown slow sales, you need to find the reason for those slow sales. The more questions and solutions for problems you can bring to the interview, the better for you and the higher the probability you will be hired.

Back to the question of how much money you can earn. Ask the sales manager how many sales counselors they have and how much did the top salespeople make last year. What is the most dollar volume sold to date for this calendar year? Ask the average sales price of the company's communities.

In addition to a salary or draw and commissions, a company may offer a bonus program to inspire sales counselors during slow periods. Ask in your interview if the company has sales contests. That is a nice way to find out if they offer a bonus. A company I worked for had a large inventory of spec homes and offered a sales contest. The contest offered a $1,000 bonus for every spec you could sell in the month. This was in addition to your regular commission. I picked up an extra $4,000 that month!

EARN EXTRA DOLLARS THROUGH LOAN CAPTURE!

Building companies are establishing relationships with title companies and mortgage companies to get a piece of that part of the home-buying process. Building companies can be paid $500 or $1,000 dollars on each loan sent to the mortgage company or whatever dollar amount the builder and mortgage company worked out in their business agreement.

If a building company places and closes 300 loans with the mortgage company and receives $1,000 for each loan, the $300,000 added to the bottom profit line gives the builder cash to invest in more land deals, plus this extra income makes the company stronger financially.

How could a business arrangement between your building company and a mortgage or title company possibly affect you?

In your interview, ask if the company has a business relationship with a mortgage or title company and ask if sales counselors are given bonuses for sending buyers to the two companies.

The next question is vital. Is your job security based solely on selling houses or selling houses and maintaining an expected capture rate of loans for the mortgage and title company? You would hate to sell six million dollars in a year and lose your job because you are not a team player based on your low loan-capture rate. A sales manager may prefer to have a sales counselor sell four million and convert 80% of those sales to the mortgage company than have one hot-shot sales counselor making lots of sales and converting none.

It could be very helpful for your career if you make an appointment with the loan officer handling your company's mortgage business and go over any special loan programs they offer that could help you sell a house.

The sales manager is ultimately responsible for his division's numbers, and those numbers could include sales and loan-capture rates. You have to ask the right questions to be successful in selling and this includes asking the right questions in an interview.

Make notes of questions to ask in an interview and take the notes with you.

After you are hired, you will be given a copy of the company's employee manual. Read the manual carefully. It will spell out your entire job description. It will reinforce what you learned in the interview. The manual reveals the company's policies and procedures. Read it!

In the beginning it can be difficult for a new sales counselor to stay focused on getting sales and trying to get the loan business. Never lose a sale over which mortgage company a buyer wants to use. If a potential buyer refuses to use the designated mortgage company, call your sales manager. If your manager is unavailable, write the deal with the buyer using another mortgage company. Tell the buyer you will present their contract to your sales manager and you will get back with them. If the job you accepted requires you to sell the mortgage company as well as houses, then you need to do your very best. It is very hard to have a 100% loan capture rate.

Besides job security another way your income could be affected by this arrangement is the discount money you offer a buyer. The discount money may be available to the buyer only if they use the building company's mortgage and title company. Now you aren't just selling houses, you are selling a mortgage company and a title company along with the house. In some states closings are handled by an attorney, not a title company.

Buyers are more hesitant to use a builder's mortgage company than their chosen title company. You will find little to no resistance in getting a buyer to close at the designated title company.

Buyers get angry if they feel forced to perform. The buyer is afraid of higher interest rates or hidden fees with a builder's mortgage company. They are concerned about the service. They will ask you questions about the loan officer. How long has the loan officer been in the mortgage business? How do the mortgage company's rates compare to the rest of the mortgage world? Buyers will be concerned about all the fees charged by the mortgage company for servicing the loan.

They will ask if it is against the law to force a buyer to use your mortgage company in order to buy a house from you. It is very important how you answer this question, and the question will come up. You will answer, "Mr. Buyer, you are not required to use our mortgage company as a condition for purchasing our house. The discount money is offered only as an incentive for you to use our mortgage company. It is our way of saying 'thank you.' You are free to use any mortgage company you choose."

The buyer may become angry and say, "Oh yeah, but then I don't get a $10,000 discount! How is that not twisting my arm?" You must prepare yourself and have all the answers available, or you could lose the sale of the house. Talk to your sales manager and get instructions how your company wants you to handle these situations with buyers.

There is a silver lining in all this loan business. Some building companies offer a monetary incentive to the sales counselors for every loan they send to the designated mortgage company. The incentive can be $100 for each loan or a percentage paid at the end of the fiscal year based on the sales counselor's total capture rate.

Or you could receive nothing. I believe in getting paid for what I sell. I also have a personal opinion that sales counselors should sell the homes, and loan officers should convince buyers to use their services.

Building companies' and mortgage companies' monetary relationship is definitely a double-edged sword for sales counselors. The mortgage money can greatly enhance a company's bottom line, and if the company you work for is financially stronger, you have a more secure job. On the other side of the sword, your job becomes more difficult: you will take all the heat and frustration of the buyer.

Realtors who work for brokers who offer mortgage services will stop bringing customers to your location. The Realtor will take the buyers to a builder who doesn't care who does the buyer's loan. That doesn't sound fair when the Realtor is receiving money from her broker for every loan she brings to their mortgage company, and yet she will blackball you for doing the same thing! Sometimes life isn't fair; that's just the way it is!

Now perhaps you will understand why a building company will put great pressure on a sales counselor to sell the mortgage company. It is all about money. And that is fine.

In conclusion, knowing the items a sales counselor will be paid on is vital to setting personal income goals. You need to make a list of the items we have discussed and ask in your interview if the company pays sales counselors on any or all of the items on your list.

As a reminder, ask if you will be paid for procuring mortgage loans, all design center options including window blinds, and all structural options.

Does the company offer a salary, and/or a draw? How often will you be paid? If you are paid commissions the month after a house closes, will you receive that commission check on the first paycheck of the month after closing or the last pay period of the month after closing?

Example: You sell a completed spec on June 24 and they close on June 30. Will you receive your commission in the first paycheck period of July or the last paycheck in the month?

You need these answers to enable you to budget your personal finances. You need to know when your money is coming to you.

Keep records of your sales and the closing dates. Follow up with your payroll department at the end of each month. Check their records of your closings against your records. People can make mistakes.

Mistakes in a sales counselors paycheck can mean thousands of dollars. If the payroll department accidentally skips paying you a commission and pays you the following month after the mistake is caught, it could put you and your family in a financial bind.

Put as much time and care in tracking your money as you do in earning it! You will find a commission-tracking sheet at the end of this chapter. You will need to keep a tracking sheet on each house you sell.

BACK CHARGES WILL EAT UP YOUR HARD EARNED COMMISSIONS

Another item to be aware of when interviewing and discussing money is the question of back charge. Back charge is a term used when a company reimburses itself out of a sales counselor's commissions for errors committed by the sales counselor or for overpayment to the sales counselor by the company.

Ask in your interview if the company back charges their sales staff. If they do back charge, ask for examples that would require a sales counselor to be back charged.

Typical examples for back charges would be advance partial payment of commissions to a sales counselor for a sale, in which the sale falls through or busts. The sales counselor would owe the advance commission money back to the company. It is standard procedure to take the payment out of the sales counselor's next available commission check. A sales counselor's monthly draw would be listed as a back charge item.

The types of back charge items you want to avoid are for mistakes you make, like telling buyers that items will be included in the purchase of their home, when in fact, you have not gotten permission to offer the item as a no charge. Another common back charge happens when a sales counselor quotes a price for an option without factual back up, or tells a buyer a certain item is standard when it is actually an upgrade. This is why knowing and learning the standard amenities in your community will help protect you from giving away non-standard items and being back charged.

COMMISSION TRACKING SHEET

1. Buyer name _____

2. Job number _____

3. Sold date _____

4. Sales price $_____

5. Mortgage company _____
    In house – Yes/No

6. Title company _____
    In house – Yes/No

7. Final sales price $_____

8. Back charge ** $_____

9. Total commission due $_____

10. 1st commission payment $_____

11. 2nd commission payment $_____

12. Final commission $_____

** Reason for back charge _____

CHAPTER 3

WHAT DO YOU PERSONALLY NEED?

The nice difference between being a new home sales counselor working on-site for a builder versus a self-employed Realtor working under a broker is the on-site salesperson's out-of-pocket money is about 90% less than a Realtor's expenses.

Builders provide brochures, business cards, office supplies, fax machines, computers, and copiers. The builder also pays for all advertising and does not assess the sales counselor for any portion of the advertising. Assistants are often paid by the builder and only provided bonuses by the sales counselor. Building companies also pay for sales counselor's health benefits, and many companies offer a 401(k) program. Realtors typically are responsible for their own health care, business supplies, assistants' salaries, as well as being charged for a portion of the broker's advertising.

The items you will need to purchase to successfully run your business are items you can take with you if you decide to leave one building company and work for another.

1. The first item I would purchase would be a good business calculator. The Texas Instrument real estate calculator is very user-friendly. I personally like the Hewlett Packard 10B. The HP10B has a few more features and is a little more complicated than the TI. The brand name does not matter. Purchase one you can easily use.

2. A digital camera is important for e-mailing photos of available homes or creating fliers with a photo of each home. I prefer a digital camera that uses a media card. It is simple to take your pictures and then pop the media card into the computer attachment and create pictures. There are many wonderful cameras available. Try some out and find the one you like.

3. An appointment book for your office is helpful for you, your assistant, and your partner. The book is used to schedule upcoming appointments, redline meetings, closings, and scheduled house walks, such as a pre-sheetrock walk with the construction manager. This is an invaluable tool. If it is your day off, anyone in the office could answer questions pertaining to any of the above schedules or make changes. A large-page book is best. I purchase the type of appointment book used by most hair salons. This book is used only for setting appointments.

4. You will need to purchase two 100-foot construction-type tape measures. Keep one in your car and one in your desk drawer. The digital measurer works well indoors, but outdoors without an ending point it will measure into infinity.

5. In addition to your office appointment book, you will need to purchase a good personal planner. Many sales counselors are using the hand held personal digital assistant (PDA). Some sales counselors prefer a paper planner in a nice binder that will allow them more space for taking notes. It is a personal preference whether to use paper or to be paperless.

6. Cell phones are convenient; however, ask your sales manager if the company will reimburse you for business calls. If you are not reimbursed, do not put your cell phone number on any advertising—the cell phone bills could be astronomical. Most building companies provide the sales counselors with pagers. Use your pager number and the model phone number on all handouts and your business cards.

7. You will also need to purchase an engineer scale and an architect scale. These items are discussed in the blueprint and plot plan chapters.

8. Items to purchase for your car trunk.
   • Paper towels and a spray glass cleaner to clean the "available" signs on your lots.
   • Rubber boots or a pair of your old shoes for rainy days.
   • A one 100-foot construction-style tape measure.
   • A rubber mallet for hammering your "available" signs in the ground.
   • A plastic container to keep all your trunk items from rolling around.
   • One-gallon jug of tap water is helpful to pour on hard ground before hammering your sign into the ground.
   • One complete contract with all addendums.
   • Your community's current sheet on available homes.
   • A full brochure for a copy of all your floor plans.
   • A first-aid kit.
   • Several guest cards and pens.
   • A calculator (Not your business calculator. This one will stay in your trunk).

It is important to have a four-door automobile and to keep your car clean inside and out at all times. The SUV-type vehicles are convenient for sales counselors but can be difficult for the elderly, small people, or children to get into. Never put car-seat-age children into your vehicle if you do not have car seats. Ask the parents to follow you in their car.

What Do I Wear in New Home Sales?

Always dress professionally. If in doubt, dress conservatively. Have you heard the old adage "less is more"? You should dress for your clients. You are dressing to make a great first impression. Dress to get the sale. Image is everything. You should always look the part of a professional. Study photos of real estate people in your local newspaper. You will rarely see trendy clothes or too bright colors on these professionals.

Your work wardrobe should be different from your off-work wardrobe. Do not mix party clothes with your work attire. I worked with a sales counselor once who wore low cut, sequin party tops under her suit jacket on Fridays to save herself time going from the office after work directly to the local evening hot spot. Dress for the activity of the day, not both day and evening combined in the same outfit.

You should be as well groomed as your personal budget will allow. You will need several jackets and a couple of nice skirts or trousers in conservative colors such as gray, navy, or black. Tan, beige, or brown clothing is also a good choice. Shirts and blouses should be kept simple. If you are a woman, do not wear low cut tops or too-short skirts. Men should not wear loud print shirts or t-shirts. Please, no denim for either sex. Denim is a casual fabric not suited for professional salespersons' work attire.

Hygiene is always more important than clothing. A clean body, hair, and nails will carry you further than a thousand dollar suit. Fresh breath is a must! Carry breath mints, gum, or a breath spray in your car and keep a supply in the sales office. Gum chewing is not a good idea if you want to project a professional look. Keep the gum chewing for moments alone in your car.

Fingernails should be moderate to short length, clean, and manicured. Ladies that wear acrylic nails should wear medium to short length and no neon nail polish. No stick-on seasonal nail art ever! Close attention should be paid to the underneath side of acrylic nails to assure the nails are clean and stain free.

Rings should be kept to a minimum of one per hand. Please, no toe rings or anklets! Save those items for the beach.

Keep all jewelry simple and clean. Jewelry cleaning and buffing cloths are inexpensive and will keep your gold and silver pieces looking new.

Shoes are important for appearance and comfort. In new home sales, you will daily walk construction sites that will be either muddy, dusty, cluttered with sheetrock dust and debris, paint spills, or a combination of all of the above. Your shoes will wear out quickly as job sites are a dirty and hazardous place to walk. Ladies, it is dangerous to wear open-toed shoes and high heels onto a construction site.

You should budget to purchase well-made shoes that will protect your feet and give them good support. New home sales counselors spend most of the day on their feet. If you elect to buy expensive shoes, then keep a special pair of "rough" shoes in your car for walking the construction sites.

After deciding your shoe budget, the most important factor in footwear is cleanliness. Expensive or inexpensive shoes need to be clean and polished at all times. Gentlemen and ladies should periodically replace the heels on their shoes to keep the shoes from looking worn down. Ladies need to inspect the tips on their high-heels. It is embarrassing to hear the metal nails in high heels clicking on hard surfaces as you walk across a room. If you are not going to pay attention to the small details in your own life, what will make buyers think you will be responsive to the small details in the construction process of their home?

CHAPTER 4

QUALIFYING AND FOLLOWING UP

GUEST CARDS ARE THE BACKBONE OF A SUCCESSFUL CAREER

The most important sales tool in your office is the guest card. So many salespeople do not get prospects to fill out guest cards because they hate to ASK for it. Without the prospect's address, telephone numbers, and/or e-mail address, how are you going to close the deal? It is imperative for you to have an open communication line with the prospects visiting your model. If you fail to obtain their personal contact information, you will cost yourself sales opportunities. Also, carding prospects will be an aid to distinguishing between "Lookie-Lous" and qualified buyers.

The monetary value of a guest card is the amount of commission earned per sale. Treat your guest cards like signed but not cashed checks. Keep up with the cards. Track the number of guest cards you take before one becomes a buyer. See if a pattern evolves. This will help you market yourself and your community. It will also help you set and meet achievable goals. For example, in your neighborhood, if you visit with twenty qualified prospects and make a sale, the pattern is twenty qualified traffics will equal one sale.

If you have twenty or forty guest cards sitting on your desk and your average commission is $3,800, then somewhere in those cards you have $7,600 lying there waiting for you to find it.

I cannot stress enough how important guest cards are to your success. Do not be timid about getting a prospect to fill out a card. Simply *ask* the prospect if they would take a minute and register as having been your guest today. If that statement is not your style, try something like this: "I have really enjoyed talking/visiting with you today. I would like to keep you posted on any upcoming specials, price increases, or discounts. Would you take a moment and jot down your phone numbers, address, and e-mail for me?" Quickly say, "Thank you so much," and slide the card across the table to them.

I have met salespeople who would not give out their company's brochure without the prospect filling out a guest card. If a prospect asked for a full brochure and would not fill out a guest card, the sales counselor would give the prospect a copy of the available homes spec sheet in lieu of the brochure. This practice has angered some prospects. Discuss this with your manager before implementing this program. Remember, the prospect could have a friend looking for a new house. Brochures are expensive, but they are in the model to be given out.

Turn Guest Cards into Money

The next question is how to turn guest cards into money. First, always make notes on the back of the guest card as you are talking with a prospect. For instance, the prospect would like a 3-car garage. They want a study with hardwood floors and French doors. They have a house to sell. Note if their house is listed with a Realtor. Write down the floor plans they liked.

It is extremely important to always write down any discounts or special buying incentives you offered the prospect. If your incentives were to change, you could use this fact to get a buyer to get off the fence and make a decision to purchase before the incentives are rescinded. If you do not write the incentive down, you could end up giving a prospect more than your original offer or looking stupid offering less than they were told when they visited your model.

LEARN TO QUALIFY YOUR TRAFFIC

Keep up with the number of visits each prospect makes to your community. This is a silent red flag that your community is on their short list of preferred builders by their second or third visit. Every time they drop in pull out their guest card and make a notation about that visit (2nd visit, asked about lot number 6). Keeping good notes will give you a reason to call the prospect. Also selling statistics will soon evolve. How many visits before the average prospect buys in your community? You need this information to set up your follow-up program. Before follow-up you need to know who is a real buyer.

Purchase a city map and track the areas in your city from where your prospects are coming. This will help you maximize your marketing dollars.

QUALIFYING PROSPECTS

The first step to your success is to be able to qualify or identify a potential buyer from someone just out looking. There are not enough hours in the day to follow up with every single person that comes into your model unless you are in a very slow area or a close-out. Telephoning everyone that visited your model is a waste of time unless you are getting all qualified traffic. The answer: narrow your work sheet of prospects down by pre-qualifying. Treat everyone that walks into your model as a qualified buyer until you discover they are not. Train yourself in three minutes to identify the non-qualified traffic from the potential buyer. This will be extremely helpful in a partner situation, or if you are a one-person office in a high traffic area. The point here is you need to talk to as many able buyers as you can in order to make more sales. You cannot afford to spend twenty minutes chatting with unqualified traffic while your partner is identifying true buyers and making sales. If you are in the better situation of a one-person office, you have got to meet and greet everyone and be able to qualify prospects quickly and move on if they are not buyers.

Who Is a Buyer and Who Is a "Lookie-Lou"?

There are only five qualifying questions you need to ask a prospect to know if they are a buyer. There are two questions to ask to find out when they will need to move. Their time frame will alert you to selling a spec or doing a build job. Listen for any of the four reasons people move.

To help you learn the qualifying questions, make a list of the four reasons why people move: job change, personal changes, area change, and structural changes. Memorize the four reasons. Develop conversation to help you quickly uncover each prospect's motivational reason for moving.

If you know the reason people move, you will know the questions to ask to determine when they will move. When you ask the qualifying questions and the prospect does not answer with a need motivated by job change, personal changes, area change, or structural changes, then you are most likely dealing with a "Lookie-Lou." Concentrate on these four motivational needs. Mentally strike each one off your list as your conversation with a prospect evolves.

Reasons People Move

Job Change
Job relocation from another city or local area. The job change motivated buyer may ask questions about driving distances. They want to move closer to their job for shorter distance and less time in the car. Job change can also include pay raises or loss of income.

Personal Changes
A larger or smaller home is needed due to divorce, death, marriage, a new baby, or children who have grown up. The personal-change buyer is the most upfront about why they are moving.

AREA CHANGES

The area they live in is going through negative changes. Or a newly, developed area has more to offer in community amenities, jobs, or schools. Once again, ask why they are considering moving to your area. If they tell you their current neighborhood is going downhill, do not agree or make a negative comment. It is okay for them to bash their neighborhood, but if you do it you will put them on the defensive. It will take you longer to win their confidence.

STRUCTURAL CHANGE

Ask what they like about their current home and you will learn if their move is motivated by a structural change. When the buyer originally purchased, houses did not have media rooms. There are now more drivers in the family and they need a 3-car garage. They need a basement. They now need a study, as their job requires them to have a home office.

QUALIFYING QUESTIONS USING THE 3-MINUTE DRILL

1. Why are they looking? (Decorating ideas, or are they looking to buy?)

2. How long have they been looking? (1 day, 3 months, 1 year)

3. Where do they currently live? (Apartment, another city, in a bad/ good area)

4. What do they like about their current home? (They will tell you the good and bad.)

5. What would they like to have in a new home? (This will tell you what they are looking for.)

To be effective, you must run through these qualifying questions with each prospect in three minutes or less.

THE 3-MINUTE DRILL SCENARIO

The front door should have a chime to alert you each time someone enters the model. You, of course, get up from your desk and go meet and greet the prospect. There are lazy salespeople out there that let the prospect wander all through the model before getting out of their chair! I cannot understand this behavior. These same salespeople would not let strangers or friends walk into their personal home without greeting them at the door. You cannot qualify from your desk!

Let's begin the three-minute drill that if used will qualify or disqualify your incoming traffic. Role play the three-minute drill with a friend and practice, practice, practice.

(Door chimes): You go to greet the prospect.

Salesperson: "Hello, welcome to ABC Homes, I am Pam."

Prospect: "Hi." (Do not be surprised how cold or distant prospects appear on their first visits. They have their guard up about YOU!)

Salesperson: "Have you seen an ABC Home before?" (If they qualify, you can later tell them more about your company.) Also, by asking if they have seen an ABC home, this will let you know if they have been looking and in what areas they have looked.

Prospect: "No."

Salesperson: "What brings you to ABC today?"

(The drill begins.)

Prospect: "We're just looking."

Salesperson: "Are you looking to buy?" Be direct! Always ask this question. It will startle the prospect into the reality that you take buying seriously. The directness of this question always brings out the truth in a prospect.

Prospect: "We're not sure yet."

Salesperson: "Where do you currently live?" This question will help you determine if they are motivated by an area change. Also this is the first question to give you clues as to when they could or need to move.

Prospect: "We live across town in Happy Lane Estates." Knowing your town and knowing what is going on in the different areas will help you spot a buyer. For example, a trucking company recently purchased a large tract of land in one of our neighboring areas and people are trying to move before the 24-hour business with the lighted parking lot is opened.

Salesperson: " How soon would you like to move if you could find the right home?"

Prospect: "We have to sell our house, so I guess in about six months."

Salesperson: "Have you been looking long?" If they answer with a long period of time, you could have a potential buyer but you will have to uncover why they have been unable to find the right house in such a long period of time. Remember too, you can have a motivated buyer, but this same buyer, could be financially handicapped.

Prospect: "Just a little while."

Salesperson: "What would you like to have in your new house?"

Prospect: "We would like to have a media room and more closet space."

Salesperson: "Is there something in your current home you would also like to have in your new house?"

Prospect: "Yes, we have a large kitchen."

Salesperson: "A couple of beautiful floor plans come to mind, that I would like to share with you. They both have a media room, large spacious closets, and great kitchens. Why don't you take a few minutes and look through our model, while I put a brochure together and pull those two designs out for you to view?"

Always have brochures made up in advance. You are giving the prospect a few minutes not to feel pressured. Give the prospects a couple of minutes alone and then go join them with your brochure.

In the above scenario, is this prospect qualified or just a "Lookie-Lou?" This is a Buyer. They obviously want a larger home. They want more closet space, and they do not want to give up having a nice kitchen. They could move in six months.

Most prospects are timid when they first enter a model, or they are tired of being bombarded by pushy salespeople and do not want to be quizzed. Practice making your qualifying questions sound like easy conversation. Your mind may be racing, but your body language needs to be slow and casual.

The most important question was: "Are you looking to buy?" They answered, "We are not sure yet." They did not answer with a no. They gave you an honest answer. They are not sure yet because they have not found what they are looking for. They need you to help them find the perfect house.

If they had answered they just came out to see some decorating ideas you should thank them for coming in and ask them to make themselves at home. Tell them if they have any questions you will be happy to help. Do not spend any more time with these lookers. They did not express a motivated need to move and you should move on. You need to be ready for the next prospect, who could be a buyer.

OVERCOMING QUALIFYING OBSTACLES

I have attended many seminars where objections and obstacles were confused. Think of an objection as a non-moveable object, or a circumstance you cannot change. Examples: The prices of your homes are out of your control to change. You cannot change the school district that serves your community. You cannot move large objects adjacent to your community, such as water towers, train tracks, or interstate highways. Now think of an obstacle as a temporary inconvenience to you closing the sale. To close a sale you need qualifying information. In trying to get the information necessary from a prospect, you may incur several obstacles.

THE "NO TIME" OBSTACLE

A prospect rushes into your model and says, "I only have a few minutes. My wife is in the car. I'm on my lunch hour." Anything they say is really an excuse not to have to endure another counselor trying to sell them. They just want to get the information and GO! Prospects with a short time frame are a minor obstacle for you to overcome. You cannot give these people more time or alter their circumstances. Your objective in this situation is to get the person's name, phone number, or e-mail address. Your only objective ever is to get the information necessary to follow up, to make an appointment, and to close the deal.

You should reply, "Oh, let me hurry and get you a brochure. If you will give me your name and a way to contact you, I would like to let you in on our money discounts!" All serious buyers are interested in money discounts. At this point, the prospect may ask, "What are your money discounts?" Cheap shot on their part. Do not give away any information about your discounts. If you do, you will get nothing back. Without vital information, you cannot follow up or close a deal. At this point, have a pen poised in your hand and say "I know you are in a hurry. How shall I contact you?"

The "Refusing to Fill Out the Guest Card" Obstacle

This is my all time favorite! You have spent time qualifying and sharing information about your community, your builder, and your plans, and now you ask the prospect to fill out a guest card. They refuse. You ask why? These are the most common replies.

1. I do not want you to bombard me with phone calls.
2. I don't want to be bothered until I decide to buy.
3. I do not give out my personal information.

This scenario makes me a wild woman. I am 5 feet 2 inches tall, but in this situation I become 10 feet tall and growing! How dare someone show such a lack of respect for my time and the profession I love? My response is the same: I take a small step back (body language). Then softly I say, "I am not an amateur. I have been successful in my career because I respect other people's lives and professions. I thought you came here today looking for my expertise and the service I can provide in the purchase and construction of a new home." Then silence.

Do not be the first to speak, let the realization of their rudeness sink in. You are there to sell homes not give tours. The prospect will shift on their feet. They will repeat the original sentence of why they do not want to fill out the card. Next, I take the guest card in my hand and say, "Only if I have important information, will I contact you. Would e-mail be better for you?" If they still refuse, let them go. Wish them luck in their home buying process and walk away.

There are too many new home sales counselors out there who do not push the issue of filling out the guest card. If these sales counselors cannot follow up, they are losing opportunities to convert guest cards to dollars. Selling is communicating. You cannot do your job or do a good job helping the prospect become a buyer if there is no communication. Without a completed guest card on a prospect, the sales counselor would be better off buying lottery tickets. The odds of winning would be about the same.

The buying public needs to be educated that a good new home sales counselor is the most valuable equation in the buying process. Never be rude. At the same time, never let anyone diminish your professionalism or our profession. The buying public needs to be trained. You visit a model, and you will fill out a guest card. Every sales counselor that lets a prospect skip on filling out the card makes it harder for the entire industry.

THE "LOTS OF PROSPECTS AT THE SAME TIME" OBSTACLE

A prospect walks into your model and you are talking with another prospect. First acknowledge the presence of the newcomer. "Hi, welcome, please make yourself at home." You can't very well leave the prospect you are with and run through the qualifying questions with the new person. Quickly size up the prospect you are with, if they are hot stay where you are. At some point in the conversation, say, "I do not want to be rude. Would you excuse me for one minute, while I give that person a brochure?"

Take a brochure and a guest card to the new prospect and explain that you do not want them to miss out on getting your floor plans and if they would be so kind as to fill out the guest card, you could call them later and share your money discounts. Hand the person the guest card and pen with the brochure underneath. Then go back to your hot prospect. That second person may or may not fill out your guest card. The important thing is they may be back. You left the door open for them to return because you took one minute to acknowledge their visit was important to you.

The "Unfriendly Guest" Obstacle

A prospect comes into the model with an invisible shield around them. They do not want to talk to a salesperson! The prospect is distant and rude. The prospect barely acknowledges your presence. You try to instigate casual conversation, and the prospect ignores you. This prospect is usually a woman.

I love this challenge! I say to myself, "Lady, before you leave here, you will be talking to me!"

First, back off! Tell the prospect you are going to put a brochure together for them and leave them alone to just look. Do not wait for an answer. You aren't getting one.

When you return, ask in your most concern-filled voice, "Are you okay?" They will answer, "Yes," or "Sure." Do not stop there. Say, "You seem almost sad." This is not how they saw themselves or what they were trying to portray to you. When a person is asked a question concerning a human emotion they drop their guard.

They may answer you or they may roll this sad thing over in their mind. Your concern has surprised them. You will see their demeanor change. Pause briefly, smile, and keep going. Say something like, "I am so glad you came in today. I really needed to see a friendly face. I had the rudest couple in earlier. Could I ask you a question?" Do not wait for an answer. "When you walked in this model today, did you get a good feeling?" Now wait for the answer. The answer should be yes; however, if the answer is no, ask why. Your goal is to keep chipping away at the invisible shield of ice to hopefully engage the prospect in a productive conversation. Now begin to go into your qualifying questions. If your office is busy when this prospect arrives, do not waste time trying to convert this person to the human race. Smile. Give the person a brochure and hope that he/she will return.

Each qualifying conversation you have with the viewing public will improve your qualifying skills. At first, running through the 3-minute drill may seem awkward. Do not stop. Keep trying the drill with each prospect. You are on your way to the top of your profession!

The final step of qualifying is a power close. Walk with the prospect to the door as they leave. This is a silent close. You are building rapport and trust. You should keep talking and smiling all the way to and out the door. Stand in front of the model door and wave good-bye.

FOLLOW-UP

Following up with your prospects is another important aspect of your job as a new home sales consultant. It is possible to sell a house to a prospect on their first visit, but highly unlikely. My statistics have shown a willing and able buyer will spend four months looking at everything in their price range before making the decision to purchase. This means they begin to narrow the list of houses and builders they like down to their two or three favorites. They may revisit these builders two or three times in the final month before signing a contract.

If a salesperson is following up with a prospect on a regular basis, the salesperson is able to answer questions and overcome any objections the prospect may have about the community, the building process, or may even be able to negotiate the final sales price. Without conversations with a potential buyer, a salesperson has no clue how to close the deal. You never know what the potential buyer has questions or concerns about if you are not communicating. It is important to create a follow-up schedule and stick to it!

Some building companies have computer programs with form follow-up letters. I dislike form letters. A prospect could visit three locations of the same builder and receive three identical form letters from three different salespeople. How unimportant would that make you feel if you were the prospect?

This is too impersonal if you are trying to build a rapport with someone. These building companies understand the value of follow-up. They are trying to make follow-up easy for their sales force. If you work for such a company, talk to your manager about customizing the form letters for your community.

A Schedule for Follow-Up

After the first visit you should:
(1) Send a handwritten thank-you note.

(2) Telephone the prospect within the first week after their initial visit. Do not use e-mail until after you have made telephone contact. E-mail is too impersonal at this early stage. When trying to establish rapport with another person you should always think, "Face first, voice second, and electronics third." You must establish yourself and personalize the relationship between yourself and the prospect.

(3) Second week: Mail the prospect the floor plan or plans they were interested in and suggest home sites for these plans. Mail these plans even if you remember giving the prospect a full brochure. The prospect, if a serious buyer, has collected brochures from different builders and will throw away most of the brochures within the first week. Your brochure could have been one that was tossed.

(4) During this same week, call or send an e-mail inviting them to come out for another visit.

(5) Third week: Call and ask if they have found a home yet. (Ask this question only if you have not had good responses from the prospect.) Or ask if they have any questions you could answer that could help them in their home buying decision.

(6) Week four is decision time for you! If at this point, in your opinion, the prospect has gone from a hot lead to a cold one, it is time for you to move on. The guest card goes into your final follow-up letter file. You will send this prospect one last letter stating that you enjoyed meeting them and ABC builders appreciates their interest in Sunny

View Estates and together you would like to help them find their dream home. Please call if you can be of further assistance. Cut the cord and move on.

Do not drag yourself down. You have had one month and 6 contacts to persuade this prospect to buy from you. It is important to note that every qualified buyer is not going to purchase from you. You may not have had the right floor plan, price, location, or home site for this prospect. Do not waste any more time. You have given them all the information needed to make a buying decision.

Some people will disagree with me about how long to follow-up. There was an old saying in the industry, "Keep following up until they buy or die." This is a wonderful example of poor time management.

CHAPTER 5

GENERATING SALES

Working your guest cards is the number one best way to uncover sales. However, you cannot afford to sit back and wait for prospects to come to your model. You need the help of real estate agents in your city to boost your sales.

HOW DO YOU GET THE REALTOR BUSINESS?

In every real estate office, each agent is assigned a cubbyhole for his or her mail and inter-office memos. Many title companies, loan officers, and new home sales consultants use these boxes to drop off literature about the products they are selling. As a rookie, I went around stuffing several hundred boxes a week. What a waste of time, not to mention the waste of money spent on printing the fliers. I was so excited; I glued a sucker onto each flier. I was the sucker! I failed to notice the huge trash can sitting conveniently next to the agents' boxes. It wasn't until about my third month of stuffing boxes with no results, that after stuffing boxes one day, I watched a real estate agent walk up to her box, pull the great wad of papers and fliers out, and begin to quickly sort out real mail, office memos, and toss everything else, including my flier, into the trash can. I stepped back and watched three other agents approach the mailboxes and do exactly the same thing. They looked for mail and memos, and tossed the rest. DO NOT STUFF REALTOR BOXES! Do you enjoy getting junk mail at your home or office? Why should a Realtor?

These four agents were not going to waste their valuable time reading junk mail. I believe in good time management and at that moment I decided to make better use of my time. Stuffing Realtor boxes is not the way to acquire their business. How do I get business from Realtors? Simple, the same way you get a prospect to become a buyer. You begin by meeting and greeting. Never send e-mail, card, flier, or fax, with information about you or your community, to a Realtor you have not personally met.

To be successful in acquiring business from a Realtor, you will need to become an expert in relationship building. People do repeat business with people they know and like.

How Do I Meet Lots of Realtors?

Going to local county Realtor board meetings is a good way to reinforce relationships after you know a few Realtors. These meetings are held weekly in most areas. Call the real estate board in the county your community is located in for dates, time, and location of the meeting. If you are just beginning and do not know any Realtors, you will find going to this early morning meeting discouraging as you will be treated like the stranger you are. Get busy and meet a few Realtors and these early morning meetings will become fun.

Creating Your Realtor Base

To get started, pick up a Sunday issue of the largest paper in your area. Most large papers have a section devoted to real estate. Look at all the pictures with Realtors as a group or pictures highlighting an individual. Read the caption under the pictures. Maybe one group picture is about the grand opening of a new office. Other pictures could be about the accomplishments of the Realtor in the photo.

Select five Realtors from the paper. Now it is time to use some of your old flier and sucker money. Purchase some nice note card stationary. Hand write a short note congratulating the person in the photo for their accomplishment. Do not put one word in the note about you, your houses, or your community. Enclose your business card and mail the note.

Wait a few days to be sure the Realtor has received your card in the mail and call his or her office. Ask for the Realtor's voice mail. Leave a message saying you would appreciate the opportunity to meet them and asking if would it be convenient for you to come by soon. Ask for a day that is within 48 hours of your phone call. If you get the Realtor and not their voice mail, ask them the same question. If they ask why you want to meet them, tell the truth: you are looking for a professional real estate agent to share business with and after seeing their picture in the paper you thought he/she would be a good match for you.

Real estate agents understand referrals. You will get the meeting. Before attending the meeting, go through your last two months' guest cards. How many prospects had a house to sell and were not working with a Realtor? At your meeting, share this information with the Realtor. Work out the details of faxing or e-mailing price increases, specials or any pertinent information about your community to the Realtor. You are beginning to build a relationship. Now go do the same thing with the next Realtor on your list. Can you imagine how your sales could increase if you had five or ten top producing real estate agents putting you and your community on their must-show list? This could be a win-win situation. If a prospect asks you to recommend a good Realtor, you will have several agents to choose from. Always give at least three different Realtor business cards to a prospect. After the prospect leaves, call the Realtors whose cards you gave out and give them information about the prospect who may be calling for their assistance.

Another excellent source of Realtor business comes directly to you. Realtors will come into your office with clients interested in the area or they will come alone to preview for potential clients. Ask the real estate agent if you could put them on your e-mail or fax list for inventory (spec) home updates.

No matter how large your Realtor pool becomes, touch base with each one on a monthly basis to keep the relationship alive and growing.

One more note about stuffing Realtor boxes: there are marketing companies that for a fee will stuff the boxes for you. If the building company you work for believes box stuffing creates sales, then you should investigate using one of those marketing companies to stuff for you. Your time is too valuable to do this menial task.

If your company encourages you to stuff boxes, then keep track of the number of sales (if any) that are generated from this activity and share the information with your sales manager.

Some building companies think stuffing boxes keeps the company's name before the real estate industry and that will eventually bring sales.

My personal opinion is the only winners in box stuffing are the marketing and printing companies. Regardless of my opinion, always do what is required of you by your building company.

ZONE MARKETING NEIGHBORHOODS

Zone marketing neighborhoods, also known as farming, is another good source available to increase your income. Find a neighborhood that is a price range below what you are selling and find another neighborhood that is above your price. People are always moving up or moving down as situations change in their lives. For example, getting a pay raise, having a baby, a parent coming to live with the family, becoming empty nesters, or desiring a better school district.

Your goal is to let the people in the farm or zone neighborhood know all about your community. This is the time to create fliers, letters, or post cards. Every mailer you send out should have your photo.

Consistently do mail outs to your farm neighborhoods. Your local library is a good source for compiling your mail-out list. Libraries have directories listing each street in the city, with house address, and the occupants' names. A better source is through your local multiple listing service (MLS).

If you do not have access to the MLS, ask one of your Realtor friends to help you. The Realtor may want to become part of your mail out and help with the postage. The MLS computer program can target neighborhoods by location or price range.

Once you have your list, the key word is consistency. You cannot do one mail out and expect great results. Plan a mail out schedule and stick to it. I mail to three neighborhoods on a quarterly basis with a staggered rotation. This means every month I have a mail out in progress.

For example, neighborhood number one's quarter runs January, February, and March. Their first mail out was in January, the second mail out is in April. Neighborhood number two's quarter was February, March, and April. Their first mail out was in February and the second will be in May. Be consistent. You are trying to create name recognition for you and your company.

SEND A FREE GIFT

People like to receive free gifts. Include a discount card or gift certificate in your mail out. Do a little research and you can get the free gifts donated. Visit with local restaurant managers and share the information that you consistently mail to different neighborhoods reaching about 700 families. Ask the manager if he would like, at no mailing cost to him, for you to enclose a gift card from his restaurant to the 700 homeowners? One restaurant I work with has cards the size of a business card offering a free appetizer. Another restaurant offers a 10% discount.

Once again you are in a win-win situation. The homeowner will be happy. The restaurant manager may get more business and I hope you will too!

The key to successful zone marketing is to be persistent. Keep trying to get your name and face out to as many new people in a week as possible. Keep sending your promotional material out on a regular schedule. Create a marketing plan and stick to it.

Ask yourself this question, "Where have I promoted myself this week?"

CHAPTER 6

REFERRALS

Referrals from your buyers can be an added source of income. Getting referrals is slightly harder for new home sales counselors than for real estate agents.

A real estate agent works with their buyers for a shorter period of time than an on-site sales counselor. There is less time for "something" to go wrong when assisting in selling preexisting homes than it is in the new home sales industry.

Another big difference is the number of people between an on-site sales counselor and their buyer and a real estate agent and their client.

A real estate agent usually deals only with their client (who is either the buyer or seller), the other parties to the contract, and their broker. An on-site sales counselor will have as many as seventy-five different skilled workers in the house from beginning to completion. If any one of these workers makes a noticeable mistake, the buyer will be at the sales counselor's door demanding answers.

At the time of purchase, your buyers may love you! Four months later they may barely speak to you. If the buyer's building experience is a happy one, you will have no problem in asking for and getting referrals. The flip side of the coin is the unhappy building experience, which means no referrals.

The way you handle a buyer's questions and issues in the beginning will determine the relationship you will have with the buyer when and if the going gets rough.

THE UNHAPPY EXPERIENCE

It will not matter to the buyer that the sales counselor is not the person directly responsible for the problems the buyer is experiencing. If a problem does occur, it will not matter to the buyer that you are not allowed to call subcontractors. It will not matter that you are not the person responsible for scheduling the work that is to be done in their house. Also it will not be your, the salesperson's, fault that the painters or tile guys did not show up. What can you do about the wrong wall-paper that was installed? Nothing.

This is true. You cannot do any of those things as a salesperson. What you can do, however, is take ownership of the buyer's concerns. The buyer needs acknowledgement. They need to know that someone will see that the problem gets handled. The buyer will lose sleep over the problem. They will be fearful that they are not going to get the dream house they purchased. They will feel like someone is trying to cut corners in their house. Simply put, they are scared. A defense for fear is anger. And this anger will be directed at you!

There are few building errors made during construction that cannot be corrected. A house is just a bunch of sticks and stones. No matter what the problem, stay calm. Do not agree with the buyer that the problem is ABC Builders' fault. Do not agree that the work is sloppy or incorrect. Do not start giving out corporate managers' phone numbers.

Instead, you should reinforce again that the buyer made a good decision when they selected ABC Builders to construct their home. Remind the buyer that you will get the information to your on-site builder and he will investigate and get back with them.

How Did Your Buyer Go from Great Guy to Jerk?

The answer is simple: you created him out of ignorance.

If during the building process you encounter an irate buyer who is out of control over construction issues, missed completion dates, or any building issue, you deserve any flack the buyer may throw your way because you failed to do your job correctly on the day of signing the contract!

You are the person responsible for setting the buyers' expectations. They look to you for guidance. It is your responsibility to give them the full picture. Part of your job is handling the stress that comes with building. You understand the building process and that's why dealing with problems is less stressful for you. The buyer is building one house. You sell more houses in one month than most buyers will own in a lifetime. They trust you to tell them about the bumps in the road before they get in the car! An informed buyer is capable of handling issues that may come along. An uninformed buyer becomes the irate, angry customer who will never give you a referral.

How to Have Happy Referring Buyers

On the day you sit down with a buyer and write a contract, it is your responsibility to explain the entire building process to the buyer. You should cover in this conversation that there will be delays due to weather, craftsmen could make mistakes, but mistakes can and will be corrected.

Cover a few common mistakes with the buyer, such as tile being laid straight when it should be placed on the diagonal. Follow your examples of common errors with the statement, "This can be corrected." Wallpaper being installed in the wrong bath. "This can be corrected."

Calmly express to the buyer that houses are man-made. Human errors will occur. The mistakes can be corrected. Go over your company's procedure for handling construction issues. Who does the buyer contact? Is there a form for the buyer to fill out? What happens if the buyer discovers a problem on the weekend?

Reinforce to the buyer that they made a good business decision when they selected ABC Builders to construct their home. Assure the buyer that ABC Builders will work hard not to have errors, but if something should happen during the building process, ABC Builders will address the issues in a timely manner.

Never forget, you were the first person with ABC Builders that the buyer met. You are the first line of contact when a buyer experiences a problem in the building process. You will be the first person to hear of their problems. Do not ignore or brush off a buyer.

You may know the problem the buyer is calling about is easily corrected and no big deal. You may quickly get off the phone with the buyer and jot down a note to yourself to discuss the buyer's issue with the on-site builder. Wrong! This is when the buyer needs acknowledgement and reassurance. A buyer does not live with construction on a daily basis as you do. You should remind the buyer of discussing construction issues with them at the time of contract. Assure the buyer that you will get the information about their concerns to the on-site builder.

Tell the buyer you will go see the house and you will report your findings to the on-site builder, and he will be calling the buyer to discuss the issues. Do not tell the buyer the builder will call at a specific time. You do not know what the builder has scheduled. And believe me, if you say he will call at 10:00 A.M., the buyer will be sitting by the phone at 9:59, and when the builder does call the buyer, they will have a chip on their shoulder and give the guy a hard time because he failed to do something he knew nothing about.

Next, get into your car and go to the buyer's house. See first hand what the buyer is calling about. Check the buyer's file; if the problem is over tile, paint, or wallpaper, read the buyer's option selection sheets. Was the installation really incorrect or after seeing the item installed, did the buyer just not like the selections they made? If this is the case, a buyer will say, "I only saw a small sample. I really could not tell what it would look like installed. I am not accepting that item and I will not sign off on my house!"

No building company is responsible for a buyer's color selection mistakes. Do not argue or agree with the buyer about the items in question. The on-site builder will walk the house with the buyer and discuss the buyer's selection sheets with them.

If the colors are that awful, the company may agree to replace the item at the buyer's expense. An example I experienced was a buyer who selected a dark mustard gold exterior trim paint. The buyer's house had white mortar, and light brick with white cast stone touches. The gold paint did look awful. The company I worked for allowed the buyer to reselect the exterior trim paint and charged the buyer the building company's cost to repaint. There is always a solution. It is not your job to offer the solutions. You gather the facts and let upper management present the solution.

Remember, your first allegiance is to ABC Builders. Do not blindly agree with the buyer before investigating the issue. Do not tell the buyer ABC will rip everything out and fix it! Do not offer solutions if you do not have the authority. You could be back charged for promising things you cannot deliver.

GETTING REFERRALS

Earlier in this chapter I mentioned that there are 75 or more people between you and your buyer. You cannot control the actions of 75 or more people. The best way to get referrals from a buyer of new home construction is to ask for the referrals at the time of contract.

People enjoy helping people they like. On the day of contract, the buyers are extremely happy. You are their favorite salesperson. You are wonderful! You are helping them get their dream house!

After completing the contract and all its forms, ask your buyers if they were happy with your services, and would they recommend you to their friends? If they say yes, smile, and ask if they could take one more minute and fill out a "Choose your neighbor" form. The "Choose your neighbor" form should be in two formats: a postcard for mail outs and on letter-sized paper to be used at contract.

You need to have the "Choose your neighbor" program approved by your sales manager before discussing with a buyer.

A "Choose your neighbor" is a referral program for buyers to receive a $500 gift certificate from the local building supply store, furniture store, department store, or grocery store as a "Thank You" from ABC Builders. If the friend they recommend purchases an ABC home, the buyer will receive a gift certificate after their referral closes. Emphasize how you would like to help your buyer get a $500 gift certificate.

This is also a good program to use in your community as a quarterly mail out to the homeowners. I send postcards. Most people classify their mail as bills, personal letters, or junk mail. Junk mail gets flipped into the trash unopened. Postcards are junk mail that gets read because the message is easily seen.

Business cards are a great sales tool when prospecting for potential buyers or when asking for referrals. A business card without a photo of you on it is worthless. People in the real estate industry, whether real estate agents or new home sales counselors, need to view their business cards as sales tools. A good business card will tell the person receiving the card who they will be doing business with, what the business is about, and how to reach the person on the card.

I asked a marketing manager with a large advertising firm in Dallas, Texas, why her company discouraged sales counselors having their photo on business cards. Her reply was her firm felt photos on a card created an unprofessional image. I agree the support teams of a company do not need their photos on business cards. But a person in the first line of selling a product or presenting a company needs their photo on the business card. Buyers purchase from the individual not the company. The individuals who make up the body called "company" build the company's reputation.

Salespeople are drilled on the importance of making a good first impression. Top producers know the first thing to sell is themselves. A business card with a good photo of yourself can make you money.

In new home sales for example, prospects will visit eight or nine builders in one weekend. After receiving a brochure from an on-site salesperson, the prospects will throw the brochure in the back seat of their car along with the rest of the brochures collected that day. When the prospects get home and have time to look through the brochures, sometimes the houses and communities they visited begin to blend together. They cannot remember if the house they liked with the green shutters was an ABC home or an XYZ home. They may not remember your model, but if your business card has your picture on it, you have a chance they will remember you! The prospects could, on the other hand, pick up a business card with no picture and say, "Do you remember someone named Sally Sales?"

To use your business cards to prospect for buyers or to ask for referrals, you have to give out the cards on a daily basis. You need to set goals. The first week give out five cards daily and work up to giving out ten cards every day.

When I make a bank deposit, I include my business card. I leave business cards lying on the countertop in restaurant bathrooms. I leave a business card inside the menu cover. When I pay the check, along with the tip I leave a business card. I give stacks of my business cards to my friends and family.

A great place to leave your business card is in the grocery store next to the free real estate magazines. I leave business cards on top of newspaper box stands. If you go to the doctor, dentist, or hairdresser, leave some of your cards in the waiting area.

When following up with prospects that visited your model, the first thing you do is to send the prospect a thank you note with your business card enclosed. They see your photo and will usually remember everything about you, your model, and your company.

How will the public know you are in new home sales if you don't tell them? Stop waiting on buyers to come in the door. Go out and prospect. All you need is a good business card.

Referral is definitely a topic you will want to discuss in your interview. Ask the sales manager how many of the closings in the previous year were from referrals? If he does not know, send up a red flag. This could be a company with many construction issues and because of this buyers will not refer their friends and family. This could be a company with poor customer service after the buyer closes.

Call several Realtors in your area and ask if they would refer buyers to ABC Homes. If they say no, ask why. To be successful in new home sales, you need to know the positive and negative images reflected by your company. A Realtor may have had one bad experience. Ask if she will give you a chance to change her mind about ABC Homes. If the Realtor says they would refer a buyer to ABC Homes, ask if they are currently working with a buyer in your price range. Keep this Realtor's card handy and include her in all your updates.

How do you get a referral? You ask for it!

CHAPTER 7

OBJECTIONS

I have been to many seminars for new home sales counselors and the topic "Objections" was glazed over. The speakers covered topics such as, "How to Get a Prospect Who Is in a Hurry to Stop and Talk." Or my all time favorite: "Overcoming the Phrase, 'I'm Just Looking.'" Please don't waste my time with these namby-pamby excuses for objections. These are actually qualifying obstacles, not buying objections. I needed help. I went to these seminars with great expectations. I worked in several neighborhoods with major issues for a buyer to overcome. I was hoping to leave a seminar with something I could use to make sales. It never happened.

So I put together what I consider to be five of the toughest objections for selling houses. I hope you will find the answers to help you sell in difficult situations.

FIVE TOUGHEST OBJECTIONS

OBJECTION NUMBER ONE: LOTS ARE TOO SMALL

Traditional single-family residences are becoming more expensive to build due to the scarcity of desirable home sites in prime locations. As cities grow, land becomes scarcer, driving the cost of land and construction up. The land developer will charge a building company for each lot in a community. If a lot cost the builder $65,000, the builder will pass the lot cost along to the consumer in the price of the home. More simply said, the cost of the land determines the price the building company must charge for the houses to make a profit.

Buyers complain that the lots are too small because building companies are getting greedy. Never let this statement go unanswered. You must convert this person into an understanding buyer! Simply answer, land is expensive. Pause after that statement and let the buyer absorb the message. Do not agree with the buyer. Do not even say, yes, they are small. Just continue with, "Yes, land is expensive, and if the developer had made these lots 100 feet wide instead of 60 feet wide, then the cost of your home would be much, much higher."

Let's put this land issue into our own pockets. Think of it this way, if you owned a tract of land and wanted to develop it for residential construction, you would, of course, want top dollar for your land. Would you be happy dividing your land into ten large home sites to be sold for $65,000 each or creating 20 home sites out of the same tract of land selling each for $65,000? It is not greed, it is just good business sense.

You need to acquire an appreciation for the home sites that your company has purchased. Be enthusiastic about the product you are selling and people will eagerly buy from you.

OBJECTION NUMBER TWO: UNDESIRABLE OBJECTS

This is always a tough one. Your community is adjacent to an undesirable object, such as a water tower, railroad tracks, graveyards, or apartments. It doesn't matter what the object is, treat them all the same. If you can see the undesirable object, then NEVER apologize for it.

If your prospect saw the object, parked his car, and still came into your model, then the object is not an objection to this buyer. If it were, he would have kept driving. If the buyer complains about the object, he is looking for reassurance to buy in your neighborhood.

The buyer will say something like, "I don't know about that water tower." You should answer, "They are all over town. Water towers provide a service to our lives." Immediately go into your sales routine, asking what size home they are looking for, etc. Your goal is to acknowledge the object and move on. You sell houses, not water towers.

If the object is a train, you need to know the schedule. How many times does the train go by in a day? Does the train blow its whistle? You must have the answers to the questions. Answer honestly and do not elaborate. The more you expound on the object, the larger it becomes. Answer the question and go immediately into your sales pitch.

I was once asked by a prospective buyer if I would purchase a home that backed up to a railroad track. I answered, "That is a very good question. I make my living selling houses. There are 24 home sites in this community that back up to the railroad tracks. I would never have taken this neighborhood if I thought my income would be adversely affected by the railroad. I am excited to be here, and I will sell all 24 of those home sites."

OBJECTION NUMBER THREE: YOUR HOUSES COST TOO MUCH

Never apologize for cost. Do not agree with the buyer. They want you to tell them why they would pay more. Explain the value in your homes. People will pay more for quality and good service.

Create value by knowing your product and your competition. Do some legwork. Go visit the houses of your competition. Check out your competition's houses in all stages. Take notes and make a comparison with your company's homes. Make an appointment with your on-site builder to walk the houses together. Look hard for construction differences. Are there differences in how your company and the competition brace the corners of a house? Look for framing issues such as I-joist versus webb truss. Does your company use anchor bolts?

The point I am trying to make here is YOU are the answer to your success. It will take preparation on your part to overcome any objection. After spending time with the on-site builder, make an appointment with your sales manager and ask him/her to help you with your value statement.

OBJECTION NUMBER FOUR: SQUARE FOOT BUYERS

First, you need to understand a square foot buyer. Ask why square footage is so important to them. Realtors are big advocates of the square foot purchase method. This method works okay in the used home market because sometimes the only comparison between one used home and another is the size of rooms. It is easier to sell square footage. You can see it. It takes real selling to point out why a smaller home costs more.

Many salespeople use the car example because it works. They tell prospects that buying houses by the square foot is like buying a car by the pound. If a Chevy weighs the same as a BMW, yes, you would have two cars of the same weight and that's where the comparison would end. The quality of construction and the interior amenities create true value. Tell buyers they can see, touch, and feel the value in your homes. Anyone can build a 4,000 sq. ft. stripped down box. Buyers compare. Sell the value and you will create sizzle!

OBJECTION NUMBER FIVE: YOUR COMPETITION IS GIVING AWAY MORE MONEY

Competition among builders is tough. We are all vying for the same customers' business. Building companies are offering buyers special incentives to buy their house. This money is called many things: discretionary, builder discount, bonus money, or builder incentive.

Examples of discretionary:
- Seller to pay title policy
- Seller to pay Loan Origination Fee (LOF)
- Seller to provide $5,000 for buyer to use for options & upgrades or

take off the sales price. (A note here, always try to get your buyers to take the discount in options. Your company has a profit margin built into options). For example: If a buyer takes $5000 in options and the company has a 30% markup, then the company has really given $3,500 dollars. But if the buyer takes $5,000 off the price, that is dollar for dollar.

Now let's answer the prospective buyer's statement. "Why is your competitor giving away $10,000 and you are giving only $5,000?"

Ask a question back to the buyer. "Why do you think they have to do that?"

The buyer was prepared for you to be nervous and start talking fast. Most salespeople start rattling off their standard amenities. Slow down. You are talking about money. Ask the buyer if they have a few minutes. This is where the footwork you did earlier will now save you. You are aware of what your competitor does not have to offer. Get a pen and piece of paper. Begin as though you are in deep thought. "Oh yes, I remember that builder has laminate countertops. We offer Corian." Approach the amenities in a negative for the competitor versus your positives. They do not have full sod. We do. Work through your amenities until you have a value equal to or greater than the competitors give away.

Let's make this tougher. Your competition's standard amenities are similar to yours. Your house prices are comparable to the competitor's prices. It appears they have money to burn! Slow down or you will burn up the opportunity to sell this prospect. Think. Dig deeper. What does your company do behind the scenes to build a better house? What do you know about the competitor's customer service? Compare your company's customer service to the competition. Never bash your competition just give the prospect true facts. Suggest to the prospect that he visit one of your company's completed neighborhoods and talk to the residents asking about their experience with the builders and the service after they closed. Suggest to the prospect he do the same thing with the competition. Will that extra $5,000 mean anything after the buyer closes and there is poor service on warranty issues? Has your company won any local or national awards? Buyers brag about their builder's awards to their friends. However, an award does not compare in a buyer's mind to an extra $5,000! Ask the buyer how they were planning on spending that money.

Maybe they were going to add design center options. Keep asking questions. Maybe they want to spend the money on a structural item like a media room. Ask if they would give you 24 hours before making their buying decision.

Talk to your sales manager. In options you are really talking about $3,500 out of pocket money for your company. Sometimes you do have to give a little to make the sale. Get creative and brainstorm with your sales manager.

How do you overcome objections? The answer is found in one word: PREPARATION. The best salespeople think up scenarios before they happen and have solutions ready.

CHAPTER 8

THE CONSTRUCTION PROCESS

As a salesperson, I found reading about construction to be very boring. I spent hours in the library reading about the building process. I discovered list after list of construction terminology. I read about floor joists, headers, rafters, and foundations, enough building terminology to put a room full of people to sleep. It was boring. I had trouble concentrating. Then I realized I could not connect the written words to people. I am a salesperson; my business is about people. Each article I read about construction was written without any human element. For sales, construction is about new beginnings. It is about construction stages a buyer will experience during the building process. That's how a salesperson should sell it. It means nothing to a buyer for a salesperson to rattle off a list of building terminology. The buyer needs to know how they will be personally affected by those terms.

We already know most buyers are visual and buying is an emotional experience. Trying to sell a bunch of construction jargon isn't going to work. As a salesperson you need to have a good, clear understanding of the building process. The homebuyer will expect you to deliver this information to them in simple terms. Construction should be explained to buyers as a simple journey, step by step.

Construction interpretation for sales and buyers is less complicated than the detailed instructions needed to build. As I said before, buyers need to see an object as it actually looks. Buyers buy what they can see. They need a three-dimensional picture. Builders, on the other hand, build without ever seeing or needing to see a pictorial sketch.

A builder builds from working drawings. These drawings are drawn as orthographic projections. This type of drawing shows only one side of the object at a time and appears flat, one-dimensional. The viewer is looking at a top view, a right or left side view, or a front view.

Just as orthographic drawings are different from pictorial drawings, buyers are different from builders. You cannot talk to a buyer using cold construction terminology and expect to create an excited, anxious-to-sign buyer. You must help the buyer to visualize.

For example: A buyer walks through a house in frame and sees the location of the kitchen. Buyers see where they will sleep and which bath they will use to bathe the baby.

A builder walks through the same house in frame and sees headers, a sole plate nailed to the slab, a stud nailed to a header, plywood spacers, crippled studs, ceiling and floor joists, and a construction schedule he needs to adhere to.

You must become the glue to unite the buyer and builder together. A salesperson needs to be able to communicate to both. To become a top producer, you must learn elementary construction terminology. You will learn to use the terminology in conversations with your builder to relay the buyers' wishes. You will take your knowledge of construction and make the building process easier for the buyers. Consider yourself a very well paid travel agent and it is your job to map out the trip and tell your customers about each leg of the journey. Informed homebuyers don't bust. If you tell and explain in advance the stages of construction, your buyers will be better prepared for the six-month trip to their dream home.

COMMUNICATION IS HOW YOU SPELL
SUCCESS IN THE NEW HOME INDUSTRY

Communicate realistic expectations to your buyers. Communicate daily with your on-site builder. Ask questions; keep up with the progress of each house you have sold.

The greatest resource for you to learn about construction is your on-site builder. He wants you to ask questions. He needs you to learn.

It is important to keep your buyers informed about the construction process. Take the time to explain the stages of construction to each new buyer. Building is a process as is anything in life, there will be an unfolding, as roses begin as buds and in time unfold into their full beauty, as a baby will crawl before he walks and walk before he can run. This is true in the construction process. You start at the beginning, with a vacant lot, a pile of wood, and some concrete, and each step of construction brings you closer to the finished product a home.

Let's begin with the day of contract. It is critical that you communicate the building process on the day of contract. Set the new homeowners' expectations on day one. The buyers have selected a lot and a floor plan and you have successfully negotiated the contract. Everyone is all smiles. The buyers have become homeowners and the lot is now a home site.

The homeowners' expectations will be something along these lines: "Today we purchased a new house! Our builder will begin construction tomorrow, and in a few months we will move into our dream home." Slow them down! You should inform the buyers they might not see any activity on their home site for several weeks.

Take the time to explain the building process, or day two of this purchase agreement will be the beginning of a stressful journey for you, the on-site builder, and the new homeowner!

Communication is the key to your success. Communication will create referral business for you and your company.

THE BUILDING PROCESS IN STAGES

At the time of contract, before you begin to explain the steps of construction, THANK the homeowners for selecting your company to build their home. Then say something along these lines: "Mr. And Mrs. Homeowner, we appreciate the confidence you have shown in ABC Builders by selecting our company to build your new home. We want to keep your confidence through the building process and to do this, we feel communication and the sharing of knowledge is vital. May I take a few more minutes of your time to explain the stages of construction? Unlike a mystery movie, when building a house, you need to know what happens next!"

This is the time you point out to the buyers where delays could occur due to weather, inspections or the buyers being slow to make selections. The first four stages of construction are where most delays occur.

STAGE ONE

Explain to the buyers their home site will look just as it does on the day of contract during stage one. Although no physical activity is happening to their home site, there is much activity behind the scenes.

The corporate office will have the house plan the buyers selected, with their changes, re-created into working blueprints. It could take several weeks to get the blueprints drawn and out into the field to the on-site construction manager. The buyers will need to make color selections and, more important, brick and cabinet selections during this time period. Brick and cabinets take 8 to 12 weeks for delivery, making ordering these items early critical to assure the buyers get the brick and cabinets of their choice. Buyers hold up the building process more often than inclement weather. The builder can do nothing without the buyers' final decisions.

While waiting on the buyers' specific plans and their selections, the builder is obtaining a building permit from the city. In some areas the permit process is anywhere from a few days to several weeks.

Stage Two

The on-site builder has received the buyers' blueprints and a permit from the city. The next step is to have a pre-construction meeting with the buyers and the on-site construction manager. It is advisable for the salesperson to sit in on this first vital meeting. Buyers are always confused about what is standard and what is an option. Your being there can help the builder move the pre-construction meeting along and clear up any questions for the new buyer. Be quiet and let the on-site builder conduct this meeting.

During the pre-construction meeting, also called a red line meeting, the buyers will sign off on the blueprints acknowledging and accepting the elevation, the location of the house drawn on the home site plot plan and acceptance of the blueprints as drawn. A red line meeting can last between one and four hours. The time will depend on the number of changes made to the plans.

The on-site builder will go through each room of the house on the blue prints with the buyers. The buyers will select locations for telephone jacks, TV cable outlets, surround sound, and security. This is the time for the buyers to make final decisions about the construction of their house. The type of flooring the buyers are selecting will be critical at this point for the on-site builder to know. It is not necessary for the buyers to have made all color selections, only the type of flooring surfaces. They will need to identify which surface areas are to have tile, carpet, or wood. The on-site builder needs to know if flooring butting up to a staircase or cabinets is to be nail-down wood. Nail-down wood would require an inch and a half space to fit the wood under the cabinets and staircase. Tile floors or glue-down-wood floors do not require this extra space.

Upgraded items that the buyers selected or important notes about the construction of the house are to be put in writing on a form called a change order. Items that would be on this first change order would be built-ins, glass block windows, and adding or deleting windows or doors. What structural options are to be included in the house? Did the buyers purchase the optional media room? Did they extend or enlarge the garage? Are there any plumbing additions like a wet bar? Each and every aspect of the house will be discussed. When the meeting is over, the on-site builder will have the information needed to build a house according to the working blueprints and the buyers' change orders. After the red line meeting, no structural changes should be allowed. Major changes cause major delays! Major delays will hold up your paycheck.

STAGE THREE

We will be building a home using a post-tension slab. A post-tension system is a foundation that is engineered for specific soil conditions of a neighborhood, based on soil boring tests or nuclear density compaction tests. The engineered design specifies beam depth and width as well as cable spacing. The system of cables is suspended in the 4-inch to 8-inch thick concrete slab and in the beams. The cables are hydraulically stressed/pulled to about 33,000 pounds of tension many days after the slab is poured. Some builders pull 8 to 10 days after the concrete is poured and some wait 28 to 30 days.

LET'S BEGIN CONSTRUCTION!

BENCH THE LOT
It is critical to have a solid, level foundation. Imagine what a house would look like if one side of the foundation were lower than the other side. This unleveled surface would also be the source of major shifting and cracking in the walls and floors. In short, the house would tilt. The first step to ensure a level foundation is lot preparation. The process for preparing the lot for the construction of a home is called excavation or benching. The lot will be surveyed, and stakes will be placed in the exact four corners of the house.

When excavating/benching for the slab pad, the builder will use a tractor or a Bobcat to remove debris, vegetation, and to level the soil. This is a very important first step; the builder will be adding soil or cutting down to create a level finished grade. The builder is trying to accomplish two things in the benching process to ensure proper drainage away from the house and to create a solid, level surface to begin construction. Inform your buyers that weather could delay benching the lot.

Forms

Typically 2 x 10 lumber turned on its side is used to form the exterior footprint of the house. The forms create the perimeter of the slab. A trench/footing is then dug below the 2 x 10 lumber. The footing is 24–30 inches deep.

Grade beams are installed a specified number of feet apart depending on the load-bearing walls and the engineer's calculations for the post-tension slab. At this point most builders will have professional surveyors double-check to make sure the house is within the building lines and the foot-print of the foundation matches the blueprints.

Plumbing Rough In

This is a really messy stage unless you are fond of mud. Workers with shovels and a backhoe will dig trenches for the plumbing and PVC drainage lines. Copper water lines are added and identified with red and blue plastic paper. If the kitchen island is going to have a downdraft it is placed in the slab. This is a good time to make sure the floor plug your buyer wants in his/her family room has been added. Most cities require a city inspector to perform a rough plumbing inspection before the builder can move forward. Possible delay could be expected if the inspector has a heavy schedule or the builder fails the inspection.

Sand

After passing the plumbing inspection, the plumbing trenches will be backfilled with a four-inch deep layer of sand. The sand is a base for the slab. The sand will then be covered with black sheeting. The sheeting looks like one huge black trash bag. This plastic sheeting serves as a moisture barrier.

CABLES

Next, placed approximately four feet apart, the post-tension steel cables and reinforcing bars are then laid front to back and side to side. They are installed over the plastic and in the beams to structurally reinforce the slab. The cables will extend beyond the edge of the slab and be suspended in the concrete slab by small Y-shaped devices called chairs. The chairs raise the cables up off the black plastic.

Prior to the actual pouring of the concrete slab, the engineering firm that designed the post-tension design will perform an inspection. It is highly likely that a city inspection could also be required. There could be a delay waiting on the two inspections.

CONCRETE

Weather permitting, the concrete truck will arrive and pour concrete into the forms. The temperature must be above 32° to pour or the concrete can crack and crumble when the cables are pulled. It is also important to note that in temperatures over 100° the water in the cement can be absorbed too quickly also causing the slab to crack and crumble when the cables are pulled.

How thick is the concrete slab? Local building codes will specify the minimum standards. Talk to your on-site builder; he knows the local code. Slabs can be 4-inches thick or 8-inches thick. Tell your buyer until the slab is actually poured there could be delays due to weather and waiting for inspections.

After the concrete has been poured, spread, and has begun to harden, finishers will use hand and powered trowels to float the slab to create a smooth surface. A long board is then dragged along the top of the poured concrete to produce a flat smooth surface level with the top of the form boards. This procedure is called screening.

Approximately two hours after completing floating and screening the concrete, the form boards can be removed. After the form boards have been removed, then the slab will cure to a strength that will support framing; this takes about 48 hours. The concrete will reach its ultimate compressive strength about 28 days after the pour.

ANCHOR BOLTS

Many cities require the frame to be anchored to the slab. Anchor bolts are used to attach the house frame to the slab. These bolts are pushed into the concrete before it sets; they are placed near the edge of the slab, at approximately 6-foot intervals. The anchor bolts will be used to attach the frame to the slab.

POST TENSIONING

As we discussed earlier, several days after the concrete has been poured, all the cables are pulled by hydraulic equipment. This tensioning of the cables allows the foundation to be separate of the movement of the soil during wet, cold or dry seasons. A delay could happen while waiting for the inspection.

STAGE FOUR

The frame is as critical to the structural integrity of a house as our skeletons are to the shape and support of our bodies.

SOLE PLATE/BOTTOM PLATE

The first piece of lumber used for framing a house is called a sole plate. Think of the bottom of your shoe. It is important that the sole of your shoe be attached properly to allow you to walk comfortably. It is important to attach the sole plate properly to allow for a strong structure. The builder begins by inserting anchor bolts into the hardening concrete of the slab. In addition to the anchor bolts, nails are shot into the sole plate further attaching the first piece of wood framing to the slab. The sole plate is 2 x 4 pieces of long lumber, which have been pressure-treated with approved chemicals that protect against termites.

STUDS

After the sole plate, wall studs will be attached. Walls are framed with 2 x 4 studs or 2 x 6 studs. The studs are usually spaced 16 inches or 24 inches O.C. (on center). This is the distance between the center of one stud and the center of the next one. Ask your builder if the homes you are selling are 16 or 24 inches O.C.

TOP PLATE

Top plates are 2 x 4 pieces of long lumber that are placed horizontally along the top of the studs. Top plates are the beginning of everything being built above the first floor.

HEADERS

When you have an opening such as a window or door, 4 x 12 lumber is cut the length needed to span the opening. Headers transfer the weight load above the opening.

FLOORING FIRST FLOOR

When using a post-tension slab, all flooring on the first floor is applied directly to the concrete. Floor joists are not necessary.

FLOOR JOISTS

Floor joists are horizontal pieces of wood that rest on the top plate of the first-floor walls and provide support for the second floor walls and floor deck.

FLOOR DECK

The floor deck (also called sub floor), is nailed and glued to the floor joists. Later, pad and carpet will be installed directly to the floor deck. The decking is 4 x 8 sheets made of OSB (Oriented Strand Board), wafer board, or plywood. Ask your builder which product your company uses for floor decking and if floors are nailed and glued.

SECOND FLOOR FRAMING

After installing the second floor decking, the studs for the second floor walls are nailed to the decking. The top plate, which is 2 x 4 long pieces of lumber is placed horizontally on top of the studs. The top plate is usually doubled for added strength. The ceiling joists will be attached to the top plate.

CEILING JOISTS

Ceiling joists are installed after the wall frames are up. Joists provide structural support by tying opposite walls together. If you were looking down into the structure, ceiling joists would look similar to the floor joists. It is all about support. After ceiling joists come rafters.

RAFTERS

Rafters are pieces of wood that create the angle, or pitch of the roof. They run from wall plates to the ridge. The ridge is the top edge board where two roof surfaces meet. The ridge may be made of 2 x 8, 2 x 10, or 2 x 12 lumber.

ROOF DECKING

Roof decking is made of OSB, wafer board, or plywood. The decking material is nailed to the rafters. Next roofing felt is used as an underlay over the decking before shingles are nailed down. The roofing felt provides additional weather protection for the roof deck.

SHEATHING THE WALLS

Sheathing is applied directly to the exterior wall frame. Sheathing paper is often called building paper and is made of a dense material similar to cardboard. Its purpose is to allow airflow between the paper and the exterior covering but not to allow air infiltration into the house. Paper sheathing does provide some insulation value. Siding or bricks would then be attached to the walls by nails or brick ties. After sheathing the exterior walls, the exterior doors and windows are installed. Now it is beginning to look like a real house.

MECHANICALS

The term mechanicals refers to systems that are installed in the walls of the house. This would include electrical systems such as electrical wire for switches, fixture outlets, receptacles, and the circuit breaker box. The heating unit and air conditioning components are set. Plumbing top out is part of mechanicals. Plumbing top out consists of setting the bathtubs, stubbing out the plumbing and gas lines.

When you walk a house after plumbing top out, the bathtubs will be filled with standing water and will remain filled until after the mechanicals plumbing inspection. The fireplace box will be set during mechanicals, and the flue pipe will be extended through the roof. If the house is to be bricked, some cities require that brick ties be attached to the wall sheathing paper prior to inspection. The framing is inspected for adherence to local building codes.

If lengthy delays occur, most likely they will occur in one of the first four stages of construction. Buyers will have more questions for you about how the house is built during these four early stages.

After mechanicals and inspections, the house is ready for insulation, sheetrock, tape, texture, interior paint, and installation of the buyers' selections. Buyers get excited and anxious as they see their selections being installed and the house beginning to look like a home.

Some builders say after the house is sheetrocked the house is approximately sixty days from completion. *Never* give a completion date to your buyers. Projected dates for completion should come from your on-site builder or from your corporate office.

The sheetrock stage is when you should meet with your buyers and make sure all change orders have been added to the final purchase price and the buyers' mortgage company has copies of all change orders and copies of checks for any monies the buyers have paid your company. This will help insure a smooth closing. Smooth closings mean money in your pocket!

There are more than four stages of construction. However, the first four stages are the most critical as they set the structural integrity of the house. I have included a summary of the building stages of construction in this chapter for you to review.

FOURTEEN BUILDING STAGES OF CONSTRUCTION

The on-site builder will follow a stage schedule similar to the one below:

STAGE 1

The start package is released to the field. The on-site builder requests a building permit from the city and the T-pole is set. All debris will be removed from the lot and a flat pad will be created. This procedure is called excavating, scraping, and benching the lot. Next form boards will be set and then surveyed for accuracy and the plumbing rough begins.

Once the rough plumbing is complete the city will make a plumbing inspection. After passing the plumbing inspection, sand, plastic sheathing, cables, and steel are added to begin the foundation. The foundation will be inspected by an engineering firm. After passing inspection, the concrete will be poured.

STAGE 2

The lumber package has been dropped. The framers begin by laying the plates and starting the walls, flooring, and ceiling joists. Next, the rafters are added. The roof decking is added and sheathing now covers the exterior walls. All windows, exterior doors, cornice siding, soffit, and fascia are installed.

STAGE 3

The fireplaces are set and plumbing top out is completed. Shingles are added to the roof deck.

STAGE 4

Heating, ventilation and air conditioning (HVAC rough), and electrical rough are begun. Security prewire is installed. The house must pass plumbing and mechanical inspection at this time.

STAGE 5

Framing inspection and framing corrections will occur.

STAGE 6

After passing the framing inspection the house is ready for insulation. The installation of the insulation will be inspected and the house is now ready to start hanging sheetrock.

STAGE 7

Next comes tape, bed, and sheetrock texture. After sheetrock completion the cabinets are installed, and trim work begins. Trim work includes doors, stairs, baseboards, and crown molding.

STAGE 8

Once the trim work is complete then interior and exterior paint and stain will begin. Garage doors are hung. Marble bath tops and kitchen countertops are installed.

STAGE 9

Tile work begins with the kitchen backsplash along with tub and shower walls. Now it is time to add the plumbing fixtures and the electrical fixtures. The builder refers to this as the plumbing and electrical trim. It is really beginning to look like a house. The kitchen appliances are installed. Flooring surfaces such as vinyl, tile, or wood are installed. Wallpaper, mirrors, and shower doors are also installed.

STAGE 10

The hard surface flooring is complete, and the house receives a rough clean to remove any left-over debris. Now the house is ready for carpet and hardware after passing a final mechanical inspection.

STAGE 11

After flatwork is complete the sprinkler system and fence are installed along with the landscape and sod.

STAGE 12

A walk through punch inspection along with a paint touch up assures a quality product.

STAGE 13

Final clean and inspection of the corrected punch items.

STAGE 14

Construction turns house over to sales and the job is considered complete.

Twenty Common Questions Asked by Buyers

1. Why are there holes between the bricks at the bottom of the wall?

These are called weep holes. They allow a small amount of air between the brick and your walls; this helps eliminate condensation within the wall space. The weep holes also allow water to drain out should any water get through.

2. How many water heaters will my house have and how many gallons are they?

These questions will be answered in your standard amenities. The number of water heaters can vary according to the number of baths in a plan.

3. What is the tonnage of my air conditioner? How many units will I have?

The tonnage and brand name of the air conditioner will be spelled out in the community specifications and amenities. The number of units is also referred to as zones. The number of zones standard for your community will be found in your specifications. A one-story could have one zone while a two-story could have two zones, meaning a unit to cool the first floor and a second unit to cool the second floor.

4. I see long vertical cracks in my brick.

These are not cracks in your exterior brick walls. These are expansion joints. The joints allow the brick to expand or contract due to wet or dry conditions and hot or cold weather.

5. Now that my slab is poured I see some cracks. Is my slab bad?

No, shrinkage cracks can occur in almost all concrete slabs as they harden. The concrete will cure from the bottom up. The black poly plastic that was laid over the 4" deep grade sand was to prevent moisture from leaking into the grade sand. This plastic also keeps the moisture in the concrete from escaping down into the grade sand. High temperatures, wind, and normal evaporation of the moisture in concrete can cause shrinkage and expansion resulting in hairline cracks. These cracks will appear as more moisture escapes.

There may also be a few settling cracks before the post-tension cables are pulled. The shrinkage and settling cracks do not affect the strength of your slab.

6. What is a SEER rating?

Seasonal Energy Efficient Rating (SEER) of an AC unit is an industry term used to grade the efficiency of the unit. The rating is listed as 10 SEER, 12 SEER, 14 SEER or whatever number is assigned based on performance.

7. What are those metal strips attached to the paper sheathing on the exterior walls?

These strips are nailed into the sheathing before the house is bricked. The strips are called "brick ties" and as the house is being bricked, the bricklayer will bend the strips down and stick them into the mortar joint between the brick. The "brick ties" actually connect the framed house into the brick wall.

8. What is flatwork?

This refers to any concrete areas that are not part of the slab. Flatwork is sidewalks, patios and driveways.

9. Why is the sheetrock in my shower green?

This product is called "greenrock" and is sheetrock that has been wrapped with a moisture resistant paper which is green in color. Greenrock is installed over the regular sheetrock inside the tub and shower walls. Then ceramic tile is attached directly onto the greenrock.

10. What are keystones?

Keystones are the top or center stone of an arch. Our sample blueprint has trapezoid shaped keystones over each arched window neatly tying the brick together.

11. What are quoins?

This refers to brickwork usually seen on the corners or on columns of an elevation. Quoins on a blueprint look like square boxes raised slightly and protruding outward from the elevation. Quoins can also be made of stone. Our sample blueprint has brick quoins.

12. What is soldier brick?

Soldier is decorative brickwork usually placed directly below the roof, around windows, or for a dramatic edging effect. The brick is laid in a vertical pattern with the narrow side visible.

13. What is rowlock?

This is also a decorative brick pattern. Rowlock is used to add visual detail around windows and arches. To create a rowlock pattern, the bricklayer will lay the brick with the end exposed. Our sample blueprint has several areas of the rowlock pattern.

14. What is the R-Value?

The Federal Trade Commission requires all sellers to disclose type, thickness, and R-value of the insulation they intend to install. The R-value is the insulation's rating for resistance to heat.

15. How long will it take to build my house?

Be very careful with your answer. Give only approximate completion dates. If you were to answer in six months around June 15, the buyer will begin to make moving and mortgage locking arrangements based on this date. If there is bad weather or any delays, the buyer could request your company to pay for their storage fees and buy down their interest rate if they miss the closing date given by you. Your answer should be, "As the house nears completion, the builder will talk with you about the final completion and closing date."

16. Why can't I run my own speaker wire?

During construction the house will go through several inspections with the city. A buyer will not be familiar with local codes. Also while installing the speaker wire, the buyer could pierce pipes or wires with nails. Remember your building company is going to warrant this house.

17. May I schedule a swimming pool to be built during the construction of our house?

The answer to this question with most builders is NO. Several things could happen. The buyer could bust and the building company would have to complete construction of the swimming pool and add the cost of the pool to the sales price of the house. Or during construction another trade working on the house could damage the under-construction swimming pool. For example, the bricklayer could drop bricks into the pool and crack the surface.

18. If I delete windows, why am I not getting a credit?

When pricing houses to sell, a builder gets bids from all the vendors supplying all the materials. A window company for example will give the builder a price for each house plan. When the builder orders windows for Plan A or Plan B the window company will ship the exact window count for each plan. The windows will arrive on-site and the builder will be charged a fee to pick up and restock the windows they are not going to use. Also the deleted window area will need studs, insulation, sheetrock, and exterior covering such as brick.

19. Why can't I choose my own roof color?

To create and promote a more contiguous neighborhood, more and more developers are selecting the roofing material and color to be used. The developer will describe in detail in the Community Covenants and Restrictions, (CCR) the major building materials to be used in a neighborhood such as brick, siding, or stucco, and the roofing material and color. The CCR is commonly called deed restrictions.

20. If my fence is built on the property line between my house and the neighbors, who does the fence belong to?

The common fence belongs to both parties and repair, upkeep, or replacement costs should be shared.

To enhance your career start a logbook of buyers' questions and issues. Make detailed notes of building problems that occurred during construction and include the answers and solutions. Keep this logbook in your office as a handy reference.

CHAPTER 9

CONSTRUCTION TERMINOLOGY

You can sell what you do not understand. You just won't be as successful as those who have studied and acquired a working knowledge of the product that produces their income. You will need to know and understand the basics of construction. Knowing the basics will aid your communication skills. With good construction communication skills, you will be able to guide homeowners through the entire building process and be able to have an intelligent conversation with your on-site builder about construction. It is vital to your success to have a good working relationship and open communication lines with your on-site builder.

I have worked for companies where construction and sales fought daily. It was always "them against us" attitudes. Believe me, when I say every day will be a nightmare for you, it is an understatement. This in-fighting has become the single most common reason for turnover in building companies. Everyone loses: you, the on-site builder, the company, and, most important of all, the customer. Do not become part of this negative energy.

Most of the fighting happens when a salesperson sells a house and guarantees the buyers of certain changes. The builder says *no*. The salesperson gets mad and now you have a full-scale war. The truth is the salesperson did not know why something could not be added or deleted at that stage of construction; therefore, they think the on-site builder is just being stubborn or lazy. On the other hand, the on-site builder thinks the salesperson is just plain stupid for not understanding cutoff periods for construction. Who wants to work with lazy or stupid people? No one. So the fights continue.

Also, once a salesperson has made the sale, they want to keep the buyers happy. How do you keep someone happy? Say yes. Yes-thinking will get you into a lot of trouble with your buyers, your boss, your on-site builder, and the company. You will make promises you cannot deliver. The buyers will only remember you said, "Okay," or you said, "We can do that."

You will work closely with the buyer for six to seven months. Relationships will grow into friendships only if you are always truthful. You must never forget you work for your employer, not the buyer. You are a representative for your company. You will work closely with buyers and always try to keep them happy and excited about their choice of building companies, but never at the expense of your employer. *Never* make commitments to the buyers that are impossible for the on-site builder or your company to deliver.

Good communication skills, a good understanding of the stages of construction, cutoff dates, and understanding construction terminology will be the difference between your success or failure in new home sales. Work closely with your on-site builder. Ask him questions about the construction process. Acquire knowledge about cutoff dates. Cutoff dates refer to a point of time in the stages of construction where changes cannot be made. Study the basics of construction and cutoff dates will become clear.

In the next few pages, we will learn the basics of construction. Having a working knowledge of the building process will improve your sales skills and earn you more commissions. Not only will this knowledge help you communicate with your co-workers, it will give you an edge over your competitors. Remember, if you want to be the best, you have to know more than the other guy.

Now Let's Learn the Basics of Construction for Sales!

Architectural Changes

The first question you need to ask: "Does your company allow architectural changes?" If the answer is yes, ask what types of changes. Will they make changes to the foundation? Will they move baths around? Or will they only allow cosmetic interior changes, such as adding French doors, crown molding, and different flooring surfaces? What about widening or extending garages? If 2-car garages are standard, is there an option for a 3-car garage?

When pricing for adding to a garage do not forget to price the extra concrete for the driveway. Will the driveway have an exposed aggregate finish or a broom finish?

Architectural changes could also include the roofline by adding a covered patio or deck. When pricing a covered patio, ask if it will have wood columns or if it is to be poured with the foundation. Will the covered patio have a floor above?

Most companies will charge an architectural change fee. There may also be an engineering fee to accompany the architectural fee. It is customary for these fees to be paid up-front by the buyers and to be non-refundable. These monies are not applied back to the buyers at closing.

Making architectural changes slows down the building process. New home communities are priced for production construction. If you add altered or custom plans to the mix, you add time and difficulty to the process. This also means added work for you and the on-site builder.

FLATWORK

Flatwork refers to your exterior concrete. This includes patios, sidewalks and driveways.The two most common finishes for flatwork are broom finish and exposed aggregate.

Exposed aggregate has the appearance of concrete with small rocks imbedded in the finish.

Broom finish flatwork is the most common finish. Broom finish can be found on most public sidewalks. It appears to have been swept with a broom prior to the concrete setting.

Another term used in construction you should be familiar with is lead walk. The lead walk is the sidewalk leading from the street to the front door. The finish on the lead walk will be determined by the community specifications. Some buyers like to upgrade their lead walks by adding inlaid brick or stone or a brick ribbon edge.

Once again, check with your company for upgrade options and their prices. Never quote an approximate cost for any option. If your quote is low, that is the figure the buyer will remember.

WINDOWS

Divided lite windows refer to windows with grids. The grids give the appearance of windowpanes. The available grid colors are white, sand, or bronze. The correct industry spelling is divided lite not divided light. You need to check your community specifications to find if divided lite windows are standard. If they are a standard feature, are all windows divided lite or just the ones on the front elevation? Many city codes only require the front of the house to have divided lite. Some cities have no requirements. Do not assume because your model has divided lite windows that they are a standard feature. If divided lite is not standard ask, if there is a cost per window or a total cost per plan.

One-over-one window simply means the glass is clear. There are no dividers, just solid panes of glass.

Glass block windows come in standard size complete window systems: in other words as a complete unit and not individual 8-inch glass blocks. The standard sizes are 1 x 4 which is an 8" x 32" window unit. Also 32" x 32" = 4 x 4, 32" x 40"= 4 x 5, 48" x 48" = 6 x 6, and 56" x 56" = 7 x 7.

It is important to understand why it will not always be possible for your buyer to upgrade to glass block windows. If the house has not reached the frame stage, adding glass block is an easy addition. The glass block window systems require special framing to support the unit. The framework for the glass block unit is wider than the frame for a standard bath window.

If you have an interior bath, dark hallway, or just enjoy light, skylights can be the answer. Skylights are quoted as 2 x 2 double dome or 4 x 4 double dome. Before quoting the price of skylights, check with your company first as there may be an additional charge for skylight "well" height over 8' tall (ceiling to roof). Also, final skylight quotes may depend on A/C load.

SPECIAL WINDOW SHAPES

You will need to learn the proper terminology for special window shapes to communicate your buyers' wishes to the on-site builder. Each shape has a name.

ROOFING

The most commonly-used roofing material is a composition roof shingle. Always check your community specifications for the type shingle your company offers. The community specifications should give the life of the shingle, such as 20- or 25-years. It is important for you to ask if the buyers in your community will have the choice of roof color or if the roofing color is predetermined by the developer.

ROOFING MATERIALS

Asphalt Shingles (felt base) are available in a wide range of colors. Felt base shingles are less durable and fire resistant than fiberglass base shingles, although similar in cost.

Asphalt shingles (fiberglass base) are durable and highly fire resistant.

WINDOW SHAPES

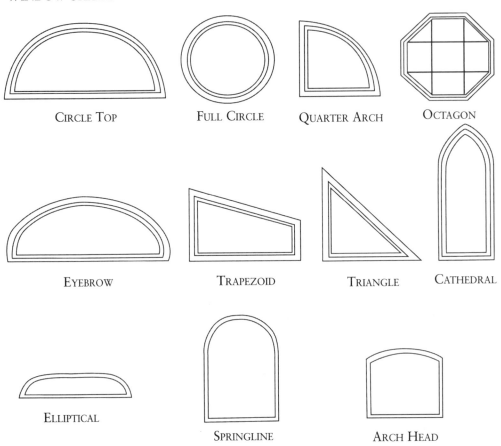

CIRCLE TOP   FULL CIRCLE   QUARTER ARCH   OCTAGON

EYEBROW   TRAPEZOID   TRIANGLE   CATHEDRAL

ELLIPTICAL   SPRINGLINE   ARCH HEAD

WOOD SHINGLES AND SHAKES

The true wood shingles are banned in some cities due to the fire hazard. There are wood shingles available that are treated with a retardant and a foil underlay. Code will dictate if this product will be available in your area.

TILE (CONCRETE AND CLAY)

The durability is excellent, about 50-plus years, extremely durable, and fireproof. The tiles are available in flat, curved, or ribbed shapes. Tile is expensive to buy and ship, very hard to install, and requires extra-strong framing to support the weight.

SLATE

Slate roofs last about 50-plus years, are fireproof, expensive to buy and ship, and, like tile, require extra-strong framing. This type framing will add to the cost of the home.

SOFFIT

Soffit is the horizontal underside of the eave. Soffits will have soffit vents placed several feet apart, or there is also a continuous soffit vent available. A continuous vent system is more costly.

ROOF VENTS

Wind powered turbine or electric powered vents are placed in the roof to catch breezes and allow cool air in and hot air to escape.

SHOWER PANS

Most production builders use fiberglass shower pans. The pans come in specific standard sizes. If buyers want to enlarge their shower, this may involve just selecting the next larger size shower pan. If the enlargement is not within the measurements of the standard pans, the cost becomes greater. The shower area will require extra framing. The shower pan will be created by using and cutting tile squares to fit the space and is referred to as a mud set pan.

MASTER BATH TUBS AND SECONDARY BATH TUBS

The first question you need to ask is what material the tubs in your community are made of; for example, cultured marble, acrylic, or fiberglass. The second question to ask: "Do the tubs come with a whirlpool system as a standard feature?" It is also important that you are familiar with the shape of the tub in the master baths of all your houses. Does the tub have a seat and can two people fit into the tub? Is the tub long enough for a person to stretch out their legs? Does the tub have a tile skirting, acrylic, or sheetrock?

TOILETS

Read your community specifications to find out if the commodes are elongated or round. White is the most common standard color. You need to ask if other colors are available. A builder may require 100% deposit for colored plumbing fixtures, because if the buyers were to cancel, the company could have the expense of pulling out those fixtures in order to sell the house.

HOSE BIBS

A hose bib is also called a hydrant or faucet. Ask how many are standard for your houses. It is important that your buyers know the location of the hose bibs when planning their new home. A sprinkler system is good, but perhaps they will have special flowerbeds that will require hand watering. Perhaps the buyers like to wash their car in the driveway. Will there be a hose bib conveniently placed to carry out this task? There is always extra cost involved when adding plumbing items to a home.

WATER HEATERS

Often building companies base the number of water heaters on the number of baths for each plan. For example, if a house has 3 baths or less, one 50-gallon water heater could be sufficient, and anything over 3 baths would require two 50-gallon water heaters. I know this is redundant, but read your standard feature sheets and your community specifications.

GAS DROPS

Additional gas drops or stub outs for cook tops, barbeque grills, et cetera, will require checking with your on-site builder first. City code requirements may demand the house have larger gas line pipes after a certain number of gas drops. A common question asked by buyers when walking a house in the frame stage is if the kitchen is plumbed for a gas cooktop.

You need to be able to distinguish water supply pipes from pipes that carry natural gas. For many years gas pipes were a heavy black corrugated metal. Today most building companies use a flex hose that is yellow.

ELECTRICAL

The common types of electrical plugs are 115-volt plugs. These are placed according to city code a certain number of feet apart in every room of a house. Next is a GFI plug, which means ground-fault inter-rupter. According to electrical codes, GFI plugs must be used in bath-rooms, kitchens, garages, outdoors, and wet areas, where there could be a danger of shock. Next are 240-volt electric outlets needed for cooktops, double-ovens, HVAC units, and pools.

(HVAC is the industry abbreviation for Heating, Ventilation, and Air Conditioning.) You need to know the SEER rating of your air condition-ing system. SEER rating is the abbreviation for Seasonal Energy Efficient Rating. The most common SEER value for production builders is 10 or 12 SEER. Be prepared because buyers will ask you the brand name of the heating and cooling units.

BLOCK AND WIRE

Block and wire refers to adding support to a ceiling and running elec-trical wire to power a ceiling fan. Block and wire prices usually do not include the fan fixture or a switch. Always tell the customer if the block and wire includes a separate wall switch. The cost to add a switch is minimal.

Electrical changes would require a quote after sheetrock, and your com-pany may decline to make these changes. It is your job to stress to the buyers how important making decisions about their family's electrical needs are prior to the construction of the home. It may sound simple to add another phone line or TV cable outlet, but always be aware of the stage of the house in question.

FIREPLACES

There are two common types of fireplaces. The first is wood burning, which means the fireplace can burn wood or if plumbed for gas, could accommodate gas logs. A wood-burning fireplace will have a chimney. Today most builders cover the rooftop chimney frame in a non-flamma-ble material like Hardi-Plank instead of brick. Hardi-Plank is a masonry fiber material that comes in a plank style resembling wood planks. It is also available in a fake stucco finish. Brick chimneys are becoming a thing of the past due to cost except in very expensive custom homes.

The second type of fireplace is direct-vent. A direct vent fireplace does not require a chimney and can be placed directly beneath windows for a more dramatic effect. Also there is less cost and more community appeal without chimneys. Direct-vent fireplaces have the gas logs included in the price and have a stationary glass panel covering the fireplace opening. There are also direct-vent gas appliances that allow bi-fold opening glass doors on the front of the fireplace in lieu of the stationary single-panel piece of glass. Buyers complain the non-opening glass offers less appeal and realism.

Fireplace openings' standard sizes are 36" and 42". City codes can require fireplaces to have 8" to 12" of a non-flammable product surrounding the fireplace box. Typically this product will be tile or brick. Check your standard features as model homes often have stone or granite surrounding the firebox. You do not want buyers to assume their home would come with the same materials in the model as a standard feature.

INSULATION

Once again you need to read your community building specifications for the standard insulation installed in the homes you are selling. Many building companies spell out the thickness of the insulation and the R-Value. R-Value means resistance to heat. R-Value is a measurement that tells how a material resists the flow of heat. Typically, attics have blown insulation of R-30. Exterior walls will use batt insulation and have an R-13 value. R-13 is also used in walls between the garage and the house. Flat ceilings may have R-30 blown-in insulation while sloped ceilings could have R-19 or R-22. The Federal Trade Commission requires sellers to disclose the type, thickness, and R-Value of the insulation the builder intends to install. Be prepared! People will ask about the insulation in their home. Talk to your on-site builder and know your community specifications. Different regions' insulation requirements will vary based on the area's climate.

MORTAR

The price range of the house you are selling will determine the standard mortar. Never assume because your model has white or buff mortar that it is a standard feature. Gray is the industry standard color, and lighter shades such as buff, white, or colored mortar are upgrades. When mortar options are available the upgrade is usually priced per 1000 bricks. Your builder can help you with the number of bricks per plan. Talk to your corporate office and find out who supplies you with price requests for upgrade mortar.

BRICK

If brick is included as a standard feature in your community, you will need to know if the brick is clay based, concrete, or some other product. Buyers will ask the name of the manufacturer of the brick. You will need to know the percentage of brick that will be standard on your homes. Is the amount of brick on the house 80% of the exterior covering? Are the brick percentages higher or lower? What are the locations of the standard brick?

Let me give you an example of one of the most common brick mistakes made by new consultants. The buyers purchased a house at frame stage. They notice an area on the house has siding, and would rather have that area bricked. You agree, brick would look better and promise to tell the on-site builder to brick that area. Now, the buyers think they will receive the brick and all is well.

BIG PROBLEM! If a house is to have brick, a 5½" brick ledge was planned when the form boards were set. The foundation was poured allowing for this space for brick and the framers will frame the house within this area. In our example the house was already at frame stage, too late to change. Now you have angry buyers. You may also have a bust. Buyers interpret poor communication as a lie.

If buyers want to add brick to an upstairs wall, this could be done before the frame stage, but only with your company's permission. Also the buyers would need to know they could lose 5½" of floor space. Sometimes it is not possible to add brick to an upstairs roof area because there is nothing to support the brick.

Communication with the on-site builder would have saved the salesperson and the buyers from getting into a sticky situation. If the salesperson had studied a little about the craft, they could have avoided this problem by having the knowledge about construction to guide the buyers through the building process.

To better prepare yourself, study each of the floor plans offered in your community and discuss brick location options on these plans with your on-site builder.

STONE AND CAST STONE

Today most building companies offer upgraded elevations with stone accents or cast stone pieces. Many salespeople have been back charged for assuming stone or cast stone shown on the blueprints is included in the price of the home. Simple rule to remember: plain is usually standard and anything extra is EXTRA!

DOORS

Sizes of doors and windows are described as width by height using feet and inches.

Exterior doors such as a front door are typically from 6 feet 8 inches (6^8) to 8 feet (8^0). The standard materials used for front doors can be metal, wood, or fiberglass. Check your community specifications for your standards. Exterior doors come in a variety of styles often including "lites," which are inset panes of glass. If the glass panes are on either side of the door they are called side-lites. The correct spelling is lites.

Interior doors are described in the same way as exterior (i.e., by width and height). It is important to note whether the interior doors are solid or hollow core. You need to know if the standard door heights are 2 feet 8 inches wide by 6 feet 8 inches in height (2^8 x 6^8). Usually interior doors are of paint grade material. The door design could be flush front or paneled.

French doors are very popular today for interior and exterior locations in the home. French doors can be single French 2^8 by 6^8 or 2^8 by 8^0 or double doors 4° by 6° or 4° by 8°. Double doors are referred to as twins and then by width and height. French doors are also referred to as French 15 lite, meaning a single door with 15 grid panes. You will also need to specify if the door is to have grids.

Doors leading from the garage into the house by most city codes must be made of metal. A common mistake made by salespeople is when buyers add an exterior door from the garage to the yard and the salesperson quotes the buyers the price of an interior wood door, which costs much less than a metal exterior door. Also, if the salesperson does not know the city codes for exterior doors, this could cause a problem. For example, some cities require all exterior doors to have a stoop and a light. You would need to collect money from the buyers for these extra items, not just the cost of the door.

DOOR HARDWARE

Door hardware refers to doorknobs or handles. You need to know the style handle (round or lever) and the type of material, (brass or nickel) that are standard in your community. Door hardware can be very expensive.

Garage doors come in a variety of sizes. Find out what is standard in your neighborhood. Door sizes range from 8' x 7', 8' x 8', 16' x 8', 9' x 7', to 18' x 7'. These are standard sizes. Also, you will need to know if garage door openers are standard and, if so, whether the remotes are included and how many.

Attic stairs refer to a pull-down unit installed in a hallway or in the garage ceiling. Check all your blueprints for attic stair access areas. Attic stairs are often an option.

CHAPTER 10

CONSTRUCTION CUTOFF
SCHEDULES

It is important to keep the construction process running smoothly. Inclement weather or failing to pass an inspection will slow down the building process. Builders expect these types of delays and adjust accordingly; you do not want to add more delays to the construction time by asking for changes that are at or beyond the cutoff stage for a requested option.

At time of contract you should make every effort to give the buyer a clear understanding of what changes will be allowed at contract, after contract but before the house is started, and once the house is under construction.

All cutoff periods for options will fall into four categories: date of sale, foundation poured, shingled, and sheetrock finish.

THE CUTOFF TIMES FOR OPTIONS

1. Date of Sale
2. Foundation poured
3. Shingled
4. Sheetrock finish

CUTOFF AT DATE OF SALE

There are twelve option categories to be covered on the day of contract that cannot be changed after the date of sale.

1. FOUNDATION—If your company allows buyers to make changes to the footprint of the house these changes are best to be discussed and priced prior to writing the contract. After contract there will be no changes allowed to the foundation.

2. BRICK AND MORTAR—It is not always possible for the buyers to have selected their brick and mortar color by the day of contract. However the builder will need these selections within seven to ten days from the day of contract. Brick can take up to 12 weeks for delivery.

3. CAST STONE—If the elevation the buyers have selected has cast stone touches included in the price, you should go over the locations that will be offered with stone. If the elevation does not come with cast stone and the buyer wants to add it, you will need this information on the day of contract. You will also need to make the buyers aware that the added cast stone will need to be priced if you do not already have it priced.

4. CULTURED STONE AND REAL STONE—Construction must know if the buyers have selected an elevation that has man-made or real stone. If a buyer is adding either one of these products, the builder needs this vital ordering information.

5. ITEMS PLACED IN THE SLAB—If a buyer selects a downdraft cook top, floor plugs, or a floor safe, the builder will need this information when requesting the blueprints.

6. EXTERIOR DOORS—Adding or deleting exterior doors will create a frame change. You want all structural changes to be on the blueprints.

7. FLATWORK—It will help the builder to know if the driveway, lead walk, or patio is being extended, widened, or decreased in size. Oftentimes buyers will add a stone or brick ribbon to the lead walk. The brick and stone require concrete support, as these items cannot just be placed on top of the grass next to the walk. In time they would settle and fall away. A concrete ledge is poured when the lead walk is poured. The ledge is lower than the surface of the walk and is generally the depth of the bricks or stone to be applied as a ribbon trim. To add the ribbon trim after the walk has been poured would require the lead walk to be ripped out and completely started over.

8. FRAME—Any interior frame changes such as converting a formal living room to a study or adding French doors to a sheetrock opening or any major frame change is information needed on the blueprints. This would also include increasing the garage door width and height.

9. ROOF CHANGES—Adding tile or metal roof material will require extra support. This is an issue to address before the building materials for the house are ordered.

10. PLUMBING—If buyers want to add plumbing to an island, rough plumb upstairs for a snack bar, or rough plumb for a future sink in the utility room these are the types of items to address at time of contract.

11. TUBS AND SHOWER PANS—Are the buyers requesting jetted tubs? Do they want to delete the tub in a secondary bath and replace the tub with a shower stall? If acrylic shower pans are standard and the buyers want a mud set pan this will affect the slab as mud set pans are set into the slab.

12. WINDOWS—Address any window changes at the time of contract. Window changes would include changing from arch top to square

top, or adding or deleting windows in the original floor plan. Changing the standard window material from metal windows to wooden windows is a cost and ordering issue. Glass block window units require extra framing.

For a recap, none of the above 12 categories can be changed once the house is under construction. You need to ask the buyers to review each category on the date of sale and have a clear understanding this is the only time allowed for changes in any of the 12 options. Once the contract is signed the house is considered to be under construction.

Cutoff When Foundation Is Poured

There is one major category to be covered prior to the foundation being poured and that is the HVAC. In most companies this is the one and only time buyers will be allowed to make changes to the HVAC. Changes you would watch for are the buyers upgrading the SEER rating from your companies standard 10 SEER to 12 SEER rating or higher. The buyers may wish to purchase different brand name HVAC units than the brand your company offers as standard. The location of the outside units should be covered with the buyers prior to the foundation being poured. If the buyers have a reason for the outside units to be placed on the opposite side of the house from the location indicated on the blueprints, then this change could require an expensive engineering redraw. It would be a possible but very costly change.

Cutoff at Shingles

There are eight option categories that will be cutoff after the shingles are complete. The categories are insulation, cabinets, drywall changes, electric changes, hardware, security system upgrade, the fireplace mantel, and interior trim.

1. Insulation—If buyers want to upgrade blown or batt insulation it must be done during or before the house reaches the shingled stage.

2. CABINETS—It is preferable for all cabinets to be selected within 14 days of writing the contract. If at shingled stage the buyers have not selected cabinets, the builder may consider the buyers to be in default. If the buyers do not make a selection, the builder will make a selection to keep the house on schedule.

3. DRYWALL—Any drywall changes such as adding, deleting, or enlarging an art niche must be made before or during the shingle stage. Rounded sheetrock corners are popular and this is the stage to check your paper work and make sure the builder has change orders reflecting any added rounded corners.

4. ELECTRIC ROUGH—Electric rough is the time to move or add electrical and phone outlets. Buyers may want to add under-counter lighting and exterior landscape lights. Check your floor plans for the number of coach lights that are standard. Most buyers want two coach lights beside the front door and most builders offer only one as standard.

5. HARDWARE—Interior and exterior door hardware must be selected prior to sheetrock to insure availability at the time of installation.

6. INTERIOR TRIM—This is the last chance to add crown molding or increase from a one-step crown to a two- or three-step molding.

7. FIREPLACE MANTEL—At the shingle stage, the buyer must select the mantel material. Will the mantel be made of stone, paint, or stain grade wood? Will the mantel be single or double in design?

8. SECURITY SYSTEM ROUGH—The house will be pre-wired for a security system if this is a standard feature. If it is not standard the buyers have this last chance to add a security system or upgrade the standard system. Surround sound is also installed during this stage of construction along with any stereo pre-wire.

CUTOFF AT SHEETROCK FINISH

The fourth and final cutoff stage is critical for the buyers to meet the deadline. If the house is not started, the buyer has up to sheetrock to make all the selections in the final category (which has 20 option areas). After sheetrock finish (which means the walls have been sheetrocked, taped, and bedded), no changes will be allowed for any of the options in this category.

1. APPLIANCES—The buyers have up to sheetrock finish to select the color and style of appliances. The key words to remember are "up to." If your builder offers a single oven as standard and your buyers want double ovens, you need this information at date of sale or prior to the sheetrock process being completed to allow framing changes and time.

2. CARPET—The builder will need to order the carpet shortly after sheetrock finish. The buyers have up to this time to make carpet color and style changes.

3. CEILING FANS—Do not get confused here. Ceiling fans cannot be added at this stage if the ceiling is not already blocked and wired. The buyers have up to sheetrock finish to make color and style changes of fans.

4. COUNTERTOPS—Laminate countertops color selections can be changed at this point but not granite and solid surfaces.

5. ELECTRICAL—Prior to the sheetrock finish buyers could still make electrical changes. If one piece of sheetrock is installed it is too late! A sheetrock company can completely rock a house in one day. If you make electrical changes such as moving an outlet you are creating major delays. All the other sub-contractors will have to be re-scheduled.

6. HARD SURFACE FLOORING—Buyers have up to sheetrock finish to select or change the selections for vinyl, tile, or hardwoods. Glue-

down hardwood floors are not a problem at the sheetrock stage. The nail-down hardwood floors require 1½ inch space at the base of cabinets and stair cases. A builder needs to know about nail-down wood floors prior to ordering the cabinets.

7. FENCES—Some builders will extend the time allowed to make fence selection upgrades and extensions. If you will make a habit of getting all selections as early as possible you will have fewer issues with the buyers.

8. FIREPLACE TILE AND HEARTH—The buyers must decide prior to sheetrock finish the material to surround the firebox. The decision to have a raised hearth would be addressed along with all other framing issues before the foundation is poured.

9. GUTTERS—Most houses are built with some guttering but maybe not full gutters. This is the time for the buyers to request any additional gutters.

10. BACKSPLASH AND WALL TILE—Kitchen backsplash and all bathroom wall tiles must be selected.

11. LIGHT FIXTURES—All non-standard interior and exterior light fixtures cannot be re-selected after sheetrock finish.

12. MARBLE VANITY TOPS—Some builders have one marble vanity top available and do not offer any change. Check with your building company.

13. MIRRORS—If buyers want to upgrade the size of bath mirrors or add beveled strips, these selections must be made well before sheetrock finish as light fixtures may have to be moved up to allow for the larger mirror.

14. PAINT—The interior wall and trim paint must be selected along with the exterior trim paint prior to sheetrock. It is easier for the builder if these selections are made prior to the sheetrock being hung.

15. PLUMBING FIXTURES—After the house is sheetrocked all the plumbing fixtures are installed. If buyers want to make a change after sheetrock finish, this would require the builder to rip out the tile work in tubs and showers in question to fulfill the request.

16. SHOWER ENCLOSURES—Once again, the builder needs to know what to order. Do the buyers want clear or obscured glass, and brass or chrome trim?

17. LANDSCAPING—If the buyers are doing anything beyond the standard landscape package, the builder needs this information prior to or immediately after sheetrock finish.

18. TREE REMOVAL—Do not wait to address tree removal. If you are selling a lot with trees you need to discuss cost of tree removal and who is going to pay for the removal at time of contract. Tree removal is in this final category only for the buyers to change their minds about cutting down any remaining trees. The builder needs to have the trees that are going to be removed clearly marked with paint or vinyl tape tied around the tree. For your company's protection, take a plot plan and draw as close to accurate the location of the tree or trees to be removed and have the buyers sign and date it at contract.

19. FRONT DOOR SELECTION—If buyers are purchasing an upgraded front door, the selection will be needed by sheetrock finish.

20. WALLPAPER—If wallpaper is a standard feature, discuss with the buyers the areas in the house that will have paper. If they are adding wallpaper to walls that are standard to be textured and painted, have these walls marked on the blueprint.

There are many more items that can go into a house, and I have tried to cover the options that can create ordering and installing issues.

You should work closely with your sales manager and on-site builder to have a clear understanding of the cutoff time periods required of your buyers.

CHAPTER 11

BLUEPRINTS

BLUEPRINTS—WHAT ARE THEY?

Blueprints are reproductions of an original drawing. The architect that created the working drawing will keep the original so that changes or additions to the plans can be redrawn on the originals during construction. This also ensures that the originals will not be lost or damaged.

I will give you a very condensed version of making reproductions of the original drawing. First a flat piece of wood is framed and covered in felt. Next a piece of paper is chemically-coated on one side and placed on the felt surface with the coated side up. Then the original drawing is placed on top of the chemically coated paper right side up. Next a large piece of plate glass is placed on top of the wooden frame to cover and seal the papers. The frame is now ready to be placed in the sun. After a designated period of time the chemically-treated paper is removed, rinsed off, and hung up to dry. As the paper dries, it turns dark blue with white lines appearing. The white lines are a perfect reproduction of the original drawing. In short, the chemically-coated paper is sensitive to sunlight, and the reaction of chemicals and sunlight change the paper to blue giving birth to the name blueprint.

This extremely time-consuming method of reproducing an architect's original drawings is no longer used and today's reproductions are on white paper with black lines. Although the paper is no longer blue, the word blueprint remains as a universal term and is used to refer to all types of construction drawings.

Lets talk about the cost of blueprints and why your company appears to be overly protective of their copies.

First, when an architect draws plans for a house, he must take into consideration every aspect of the building process. The drawings will detail the architectural design of the house and include explicit drawings for plumbing, structural, electrical, HVAC, and framing. The architect will spend countless hours creating one design. Some architects will draw the design and all mechanicals while others will prepare the design and hire engineers to design the mechanicals (plumbing, heating, cooling, and structural). It really doesn't matter who does which part as long as all the drawings are exact. Incorrectly drawn blueprints can lead to mistakes, which can cause construction delays, and delays add to the cost of construction. Therefore, it is imperative that the working drawings/blueprints are correct. The builder will hire many differently skilled contractors to construct his houses. The contractors will read and follow the drawings much like a seamstress follows patterns. A building company is paying for perfection in the blueprints. A building company will pay more for an architect whose work is precise, even if this means an increase in the cost to build each house.

The building company will purchase the right to use the drawings from an architect. In new home sales it is not uncommon to offer as many as ten different floor plans in just one community. Think of the company you are working for or hope to be employed by. How many communities do they have? How many plans are in each of these communities? Often plans are community specific. For example, the building company would not offer the same plans in a $100,000 neighborhood as they offer in a $300,000 neighborhood. Another factor that determines plan design is the size of the lots. Zero lot line communities typically allow a maximum 40-foot wide house due to the narrow lots. This same 40-foot house would look ridiculous on a larger home site. Remember too that some communities will require front-entry homes while others use rear entry.

I hope you are beginning to understand why blueprints are a costly part of building. Investing in a skilled architect is critical to the success of a building company. A building company will have a huge amount of money invested in their blueprint inventory. For instance a large building company could have purchased one hundred or more blueprints from an architect to use in their communities. The cost is one factor but popular fast-selling designs are also crucial to a company's success.

Along with blueprints, a building company will also spend thousands of dollars each year on community brochures. Brochures will have information about the community such as standard features, a site map, price sheet, and a footprint or outline drawing of each floor plan offered in the community. The building company encourages their salespeople to give the brochure to all prospective buyers. And this brings us to an important career-ending mistake.

Salespeople have been fired for giving customers copies of blueprints. Buyers assume that the purchase of their new home includes a set of blueprints. The blueprints are not part of the purchase price. It is different when building a custom home; the builder may offer the custom prints as part of the purchase. However, we are talking about new home sales and the blueprints are NEVER offered to buyers. Blueprints are copyrighted material, expensive to purchase, and belong exclusively to your company.

If buyers ask you for a copy of the blueprints, tell them in a nice way that blueprints are the property of your company.

The main reason buyers want a copy of their blueprint is for room dimensions. If the brochure footprints of your house plans do not have room dimensions printed in the center of each room, then you should measure each room on the blueprint and have that information available for buyers. When using the material in your brochures, always stress to prospects and buyers that the brochure and all advertising, floor plan representations, and illustrations are general concepts only. Also, all room dimensions and square footages listed in a brochure and the measurements you have personally given them detailing room dimensions are approximate.

Why Do Blueprints Intimidate People?

First, blueprints are orthographic projections. An orthographic projection shows only one view of an object at a time. The object appears flat and one-dimensional. The viewer is looking at a top view, as though they were looking down from a plane. Or they are seeing a flat right-side view or a one-dimensional left-side view of the house. It is difficult for the average person to visualize the finished product from a one-dimensional drawing.

Another reason is most people have had little to no exposure to blueprints. The word blueprint sounds complicated. Think back to the first time you ever saw a blueprint. Did you understand all the different lines? Did you understand the symbols and abbreviations used throughout the blueprint? Your answer is probably no. Remember too, prospects coming into your model will have their guard up about you. They do not trust you (yet). Be careful not to embarrass prospects by assuming they are as familiar with blueprints as you are. Do not yank out a set of blueprints and start showing off your blueprint reading skills. Instead, guide the conversation with phrases such as, "and as you can see, the master closet has one rod and two shelves, indicated here by the abbreviations IR2S." Successful salespeople use blueprints to help prospects "see" a house. Sharing blueprints with prospective buyers is a good way to silently sell and close. As prospects become familiar with "reading blueprints," you are helping to create a comfort zone for the prospect with the prints, and most importantly, with YOU!

The best way to help a prospect to read a blueprint is to go slowly. You should explain briefly the different plans that make up a set of blueprints. The plans are Foundation Plans, Floor Plans, Elevations, Structural Framing Plans, Mechanical Plans, Plumbing Plans, and Electrical Plans.

FOUNDATION PLANS

The foundation plan will indicate the type of foundation, (slab or pier) that is planned for the house. The foundation plans show the details of the footing and support members for a pier foundation and the post-tension steel cables and reinforcing bars for a slab foundation. A registered engineer prepares these plans.

FLOOR PLANS

Floor plans contain all information detailing the design of the house (room dimensions, ceiling heights, and location of all doors and windows). These are the plans most buyers want to see. Floor plans are a one-dimensional view of the interior of the house.

ELEVATIONS

Elevation drawings show all four exterior views of the house. Elevation drawings will also indicate the materials to be used on the exterior of the house, such as brick or siding. The elevation drawings will have a good view of the roofline. Plate height can also be noted on the elevation pages.

INTERIOR ELEVATIONS

Interior elevations will show section views of cabinets in the kitchen, utility, and bathrooms. It will also have a view of walls that have special treatments, such as a sheetrock arched opening. Fireplace location, firebox sizes, stairways, or other built-in items will be detailed on the interior elevation pages.

STRUCTURAL FRAMING PLANS

There will be separate pages showing floor framing plans, wall framing plans and roof framing plans. Often, copies of blueprints for sales will not have the structural framing plans or the foundation plans.

MECHANICAL PLANS

Mechanicals refer to the heating, ventilating, air conditioning, and plumbing systems. Sales plans may not include these pages.

ELECTRICAL

You will refer to the electrical plan often to answer buyers' questions. The schematic wiring diagram shows the standard electrical layout for the house. You will need to learn a few electrical symbols to make this easy for you to find the answers. A standard detail, also called a legend, is included in the book.

WHAT ABOUT ALL THOSE LINES, SYMBOLS, AND ABBREVIATIONS?

The language of blueprints is made up of lines symbols and abbreviations. To read and understand blueprints you will need to become familiar with this system of communication. The lines, symbols, and abbreviations help convey to the construction trades the architect's exact intentions.

The symbols used are universal, and most blueprints contain a legend or symbol list. Symbols are used to represent appliances, electrical fixtures, plumbing fixtures, and HVAC components. Symbols also represent a variety of items in a house including windows, doors, and the type building materials to be used. If buyers were to ask you if the back of the house has brick or siding, you would look on the blueprint in the elevation section. The area in question will have the architect symbol for the type of material to be used drawn in the space and the abbreviated name of the material for that area will be shown, for example, brick will be noted as BRK.

Abbreviations are used, because it would be impossible to spell out every item in a blueprint. It would also take up too much space. Imagine if the architect spelled refrigerator, obscure glass, or double hung windows instead of using the abbreviations for these words, REF, OGL, and, DHW. You will find a list of abbreviations used in plans at the end of this book. I selected abbreviations that you will use on a daily basis. There are hundreds more abbreviations used in the building industry.

There are nine commonly used lines in residential blueprints. Familiarize yourself with these lines, and you will be able to read a blueprint as easily as following a road map. Lines can be tricky as they vary in thickness and length. Lines can be continuous, broken, short, long, or a combination. Lines can be different in a floor plan from lines in a mechanical drawing. The lines will look the same but may have different meanings. For this reason, a line legend is important to preview for each blueprint. For your convenience, the different lines commonly used in residential construction have been identified on the blueprint and plot plan in this book.

The Nine Lines of Blueprints

The most commonly used lines are Dimension Line, Extension Line, Section Line, Hidden Line, Object Line, Break Line, Center Line, Property Line, and Stair Line.

A dimension line is a thin unbroken line, with an arrow or dash on each end. This line will show the length and width of an object. For example, the house is 62' 11" in length and 56' 11" in width. One dimension line would run vertically indicating the length of the object in 62' and 11". The second dimension line would run horizontally indicating the width of the object, as 56' and 11". Dimension lines usually stop against an extension line with arrowheads, slashes, or dots. An extension line marks the point of beginning and the point of end.

DIMENSION & EXTENSION LINES

Section lines are thin lines drawn at a 45° angle. They are used to separate different materials. For example, they show the interior detail of a wall or room. Imagine cutting an object in half and then viewing the cut section.

SECTION LINE

Hidden lines are short dashes drawn in medium thickness. They indicate objects that cannot be seen in a flat one-dimensional drawing. The most common use of hidden lines is to indicate changes in a ceiling as in our blueprint indicating the rotunda foyer ceiling.

- - - - - - - - - - - - - - - - - - - -

HIDDEN LINE

An object line is a heavy black continuous line. This is the most visible line on a blueprint. It defines the objects (interior and exterior walls). It is also used to identify patios, decks, and driveways. The line breaks only for window and door openings.

MAIN OBJECT LINE

Center lines are thin, not-too-dark lines consisting of a long dash followed by a short dash and repeating the pattern. (CL) or (C) is also used to identify the centerline. A centerline is used to identify the exact center of an object.

CENTER LINE

Break lines are used to indicate that the object continues. There are two types of break lines. Either a long, straight line with a zigzag or wavy line to indicate the object continues, or a short thick wavy line for small breaks.

BREAK LINE

Property lines are used on site and lot plot maps. Property lines are extra dark, thick lines consisting of long dashes alternating with two short dashes.

PROPERTY LINE

Stair line is used to indicate the direction of the stairs. For example, stairs on the first floor would be labeled up to indicate the staircase ascends. A short light line with an arrow pointing in the direction of ascent or descent and the corresponding word "up" or "down" is printed above the stair line. A detailed drawing of a staircase has been included in this chapter. Review the staircase details and learn the proper terms for all the stair parts.

STAIR LINE

WORKING WITH AN ARCHITECT SCALE

It would be impossible for an architect to draw a set of blueprints the actual size of a house. For that reason an architect creates a scaled-down version of the house by using an architect's scale. When a blueprint is drawn to scale, all the lines in the drawing are reduced by the same ratio, and dimensions on the drawing should be thought of in terms of the actual dimensions of the house.

To work with blueprints you will need to purchase an architect scale. One can be purchased at any office supply store. The scales come in varied sizes and shapes; however the most popular shape is triangular. An architect scale is actually several proportional scales combined in one. The scales are 16, $3/16$, $3/32$, $1/2$, $1/8$, $1/4$, $1\frac{1}{2}$, 3, $3/4$, 1, and $3/8$. On the triangular scale, there are two scales on each side of the ruler. One scale reads right to left and the other scale reads left to right.

The scale size to be used for a specific blueprint is noted on each page of the blueprint, usually near the bottom of the page. The notation will read $1/4$ = 1 foot or $1/8$ = 1 foot, whatever the case may be. The scale to be used is also noted in the title block box.

HOW DO YOU USE AN ARCHITECT SCALE?

Architect scales are based on increments of 12 and is an open divided scale. One end of the scale has a fully subdivided section, then the number zero: following the zero are the main units which are numbered along the entire length of the scale.

When reading an open divided scale, start at the zero line and not at the beginning of the subdivided section. If additional inches are needed, you can add these from the subdivided section.

Today most builders are using 11" x 17" copies of the original blueprint. Using proportion scales reduces the prints to sizes that are manageable. It is more cost effective to make 11" x 17" copies for all the construction trades in lieu of 24" x 36" size copies. You will find working with the smaller proportion sets is much easier than the larger original 24" x 36" prints. The scale for 11" x 17" is usually ⅛" equals 1 foot.

The proportion scales found on architect scales are listed below:

SCALE	PROPORTION TO 1' 0"			REDUCTION RATIO
³/₃₂	³/₃₂ inches	=	1' 0"	1:128
³/₁₆	³/₁₆ inches	=	1' 0"	1:64
³/₈	³/₈ inches	=	1' 0"	1:32
³/₄	³/₄ inches	=	1' 0"	1:16
1½	1½ inches	=	1' 0"	1:8
3	3 inches	=	1' 0"	1:4
⅛	⅛ inches	=	1' 0"	1:96
¼	¼ inches	=	1' 0"	1:48
½	½ inches	=	1' 0"	1:24
1	1 inch	=	1' 0"	1:12

GETTING FAMILIAR WITH A COMPLETE SET OF BLUEPRINTS

Take a set of blueprints and familiarize yourself with its layout. Each blueprint reads like a mini novel. The blueprint holds all the answers to any buyers questions.

Think ahead, what questions would buyers ask? What would you want to know if you were the buyer? Walk your mind through every blueprint of each house to be offered in your community.

Take a mental tour of the plan. Look for selling features and their benefits. Reading and sharing blueprints with buyers will draw a line between you and your competition. Anyone can take buyers to a completed house and sell them. It takes a *top producer* to close a sale with just blueprints. With practice you can become that top producer!

THE COVER PAGE

All sets of blueprints begin with a cover page. The cover page is your guide. It specifies plate height information, square footages, name of the plan, the scale, the buyer's name, address of the house, building company, and the architectural company that drew the plans. This information is displayed inside a box called a title block. The cover page will also have an index sheet similar to any index with a list of the contents.

Page one will note at the bottom how many pages there are in the set (i.e. 1 of 6). The index will list floor plans, foundation plans, electrical plans, interior elevations/details, and schematic structurals.

An important item on the cover page is the last revision date. If you are selling from blueprints always be aware of this date. Your company may have made changes to the plan, and you could be using old plans.

This doesn't sound important, but, for example, in a secondary bath the second lavatory/sink is now an option and your plans show two lavatories with no (opt.) printed above one of the bowls. Your buyer will expect and demand the second sink be included at no charge. This could cost you money as a back charge against your commissions.

Other items listed on the cover page are the square footages. They are listed as first floor, second floor, and total living. A black box outlines the square footages of the house. After the first and second floor square footages, the square footages of garage and porches for a total under-roof square footage number are listed, all within this same box. Patios are typically listed after the total under-roof numbers.

Know if your builder is advertising his square footages as total living or total under-roof. Buyers are interested in total living. They can get angry if they think the living space is 3,500 square feet when actually the 3,500 square feet number also includes the garage area and the patio.

If the plan offers additional structural options such as media rooms, game rooms, extra bedrooms, or baths the additional square footages will be listed at the bottom of the square footage box or on the floor plan page where this addition would be drawn in the blueprint.

Below are samples of a Title Box, Plate Height Information Box and Square Footage Boxes found in a set of blueprints.

TITLE BOX

Smith & Gossett Architects
567 Hillcrest Dr. Dallas, TX

Gibson Residence   Lot 12 Block 16
5834 Churchill Way Dallas, TX
Drawn: 06/09/03   Job #1612
Scale: 1/4"=1'0"   Sheet # A-2 of 6

The title box includes the name and address of the architectural firm that prepared the blueprints, the homeowners' name and address, date blueprints were drawn, job number, initials of architect, and scale information.

PLATE HEIGHT INFORMATION

1st floor Plate Ht.   10' 0" AFF
2nd floor Plate Ht.   8' 0" AFF

2nd Floor
Structural HT.   15" Trusses
MAX Bldg Pad Width   52' 11"
MAX Bldg Pad Depth   69' 11"
Note:
Plate heights are standard as listed above
Unless otherwise stated on Elevation
Drawings.

The plate height information box is the place to look when answering buyers' questions concerning how high the ceilings are in each room.

The abbreviation AFF is for above finished floor a point of reference for measurement.

SQUARE FOOTAGE

1st Floor	1948 S.F.
2nd Floor	849 S.F.
Total AC	2797 S.F.
Garages and/or storage	484 S.F.
Covered Patio or Porch	30 S.F.
Overall Width	52' 11"
Overall Depth	69' 11"

Get familiar with your company's plans and information box details before meeting with clients. Know ahead of time where to find the answers to your clients' questions.

LEARNING TO READ BLUEPRINTS

If you can identify the following items on our sample blueprint, you will be able to successfully sell from blueprints.

- Identify the brick locations on the plan.
- Identify window sizes and door heights.
- Identify how many rods and shelves are in the closets.
- Locate the water heaters.
- Identify ceiling heights and any vaults, pop-ups, or slopes in the ceilings.
- Locate the flooring surfaces.
- How many bedrooms and baths are in the plan?
- How many shelves are in the kitchen pantry?
- Does the study have a closet?
- Locate the appliances.
- Give room dimensions.

- Identify width and length of the house.
- Does a porch elevation require a 5-foot longer lot?
- Locate linen closets and extra storage.
- Locate and discuss the elevation page.
- Locate lighting and ceiling fans.
- Identify if an island is standard or optional.
- Is there a seat in the master shower?
- Identify if built-ins are optional or included.
- Locate any change in the slab.

LET'S BEGIN

LOCATE BRICK

A thin, continuous, solid black line will identify the brick locations on the house. Look at our sample blueprint and follow the line around the house. Any areas that change from a solid black line to a single lighter line indicate a no-brick area. Look at the garage for the line break and also all window and door openings. The darker shaded line indicates interior and exterior walls of the house.

LOCATE DOOR AND WINDOW SIZES

Door heights and widths are written in feet and inches within the arch of the door opening. The front door on our sample blueprint has a circle with 8° written inside it. This tells the reader the front door is eight feet tall. There are three windows in the family room, and the blueprint tells us 3°6° SH, 3' wide, 6' high, and single hung on either side of two 4°6° single hung windows with mullions.

CLOSET RODS AND SHELVES

In our sample, our master bedroom has two closets listed HIS & HERS. The closet labeled HIS has 2R2S which means 2 rods, 2 shelves plus a section of 5 shelves on each side of the closet to be used for shoes or sweaters. HER closet has one 5-shelf section and one wall with 2R2S, two rods and two shelves, plus two walls with one rod, one shelf, 1R1S.

LOCATE THE WATER HEATER

Buyers will ask if the water heaters are located in the attic or garage. In our plan there are two water heaters, and both are located in the garage.

VISUALIZE THE CEILINGS

Ceiling heights can vary from room to room. Ceiling heights are usually listed directly beneath the name of the room. For example, the study in our plan vaults to a 9' ceiling, while the dining room has a 10' ceiling height. The foyer has an 11' ceiling, while the living room is only 9'. Sharing ceiling detail with prospects is a great way to create excitement in a floor plan. In the rotunda you will see a hexagon shape drawn in light broken lines. This indicates the pop up detail of the ceiling. Notice how the ceiling pops from 8', 9', and 10' to the 11' ceiling line. Imagine how beautiful and dramatic this ceiling could be if you added crown molding at each level! Also look at the interesting ceiling detail of the dining room. These are selling points.

FLOORING SURFACES

Flooring surfaces are also listed next to or below the room name. For example, the flooring in the rotunda is noted to be tile, the living room is carpet (CPT), while the master bath and secondary bath will have sheet vinyl (SV).

BEDROOMS AND BATHS

Our sample blueprint has 3 bedrooms and 2 full baths.

DESCRIBING PANTRY STORAGE

How many shelves are in the kitchen pantry and the study closet? First locate the kitchen and identify if there is a pantry. Pantries may or may not be labeled. If they are labeled you will see the word PANTRY or the abbreviation PAN. If your plan does not list any shelves or rods in the study closet, these items are probably not standard and your buyers would have to pay to add rods and shelves. The study in our plan has a small closet with two bi-fold doors, and the closet has five shelves.

APPLIANCES

When identifying the location of kitchen appliances, refer to your community specifications for standard appliances. Refrigerators (REF) are seldom included as part of the purchase price, and double ovens are often upgrades. DW will identify a dishwasher. You will need to know if electric or gas cook-tops are standard. If an electric cooktop is standard, is it a coil style or a glass smooth top? Another important issue is if ovens and cooktops are combined in one unit or if they are separate appliances. If the location of the microwave is not shown in the kitchen, refer to the interior elevation page in the blueprints; these will have detailed drawings of the kitchen. The microwave could be an over-the-range (OTR) or a built-in. It could also not be a standard item. Microwaves are shown on a blueprint by the abbreviations MICRO or MW.

ROOM DIMENSIONS

Be very careful when giving out room dimensions. Emphasize to the buyer the dimensions you are giving are approximate. To measure with your architect scale, first read at the bottom of your blueprint which scale applies to your prints. In our plan, ¼'' equals 1'. To use the scale, find the side of the triangle that reads ¼''. Room sizes are determined from interior wall to interior wall.

FIND THE WIDTH AND LENGTH OF A HOUSE

It will be important for you to know if all your plans will fit all the home sites in your community. You will need to know the width and length of each of your plans. The floor plan page of your blueprints will have dimension lines that run horizontally from one corner of the house to the opposite corner listing in feet and inches the width. For the length or depth, vertical dimension lines will run from front to back of the plan in feet and inches. The chapter on plot plans will give you more information on setback and building lines to calculate proper fit of a plan on a lot.

PORCHES

Porches shown on the elevation page may be an upgrade option. You need to know if the house will fit onto a standard home site if you add a porch. Porches can extend out from the front door, 5', 8', or any depth.

Some plans are drawn with a cosmetic porch. The depth of the plan does not change with a cosmetic porch. This type porch is very small, usually 2' in depth or less, and the space may have been taken from the adjoining room to create a cosmetic porch. If the porch extends out from the house, check the plans for the dimensions to determine if the porch adds depth to the overall house dimensions.

EXAMPLE:

You have a lot that is 115' in depth. The lot is 75' feet wide. Your building setbacks are 25' front setback, 10' side setbacks, and a 20' rear setback. The house your buyers want to build is 55' wide and 70' long. Your buyer would like to add a 5' porch to the front elevation.

Will the house with the added porch fit on the lot?

115	Lot depth
-25'	Front setback
90'	
-75'	70' house plus 5' porch
15'	
-20'	rear setback
NO	Lot is 5 feet too short!

It is easy to do the simple math ahead of time if you have elevations that offer porches. As I said before, some porches may not add any length to the house. Study your product and your lots. Be prepared!

CLOSETS

Everyone wants to know how many closets they have for linens, clothes, or storage. Familiarize yourself with all your plans. Looking at our sample blueprint locate all the bedroom and hallway closets. Did you find the linen closet next to bedroom number 1?

WHAT WILL THE HOUSE LOOK LIKE?

Study the elevation pages in your blueprints. Pay special attention to brick detail. Does the plan have soldier brick at the eaves? Are there brick or cast stone quoins? Are there stone options available for the elevations?

If there are extra charges for any of your elevations, you will need to know the cost for each.

Buyers will want to view all four sides of the house. Study your plans and be prepared to answer questions. The elevation page will also give the plate line or wall height for the house.

ELECTRICAL

Study the electrical page of your blueprint. Review the electrical legend at the end of this chapter. Questions you will be asked: Are there switches for the ceiling fan and the ceiling fanlight? In our blueprint, look on the wall in the family room and you will see two slightly broken lines leading from the wall to the ceiling fan. This indicates there are two switches to the fan. The study has only one switch. This would mean an upgrade for the buyer to add a fan and to block and wire for the second switch. Another very common question about electrical: What type of lighting is in the kitchen? Our plan has the symbol for 4 recessed can lights and 1 ceiling fixture for the breakfast room. Are there coach lights on the exterior of this house? No. Do all the closets have lights? In our sample house, only walk-in closets have lights.

The electrical page will also show you the standard locations for telephone and TV cables. Review the symbol page. Be careful with TV and cable locations on blueprints, as there could be more shown than are standard in your community.

ISLANDS

Before discussing islands with buyers check two places in your plans. First check the floor plan page to see if an island is drawn in the kitchen and if it has the word (opt) on it. If there is an island but no (opt) check the interior detail page to see the kitchen cabinets and island detail. The island may be marked optional in this section. Once again, refer to your standard features.

SHOWER SEAT

Buyers always want to know if their shower will have a seat. Seats will be marked on the floor plan page inside the shower. Check the symbol page in this book to identify showers. Shower seats can also be an upgrade. It takes extra framing and tile to create a seat.

BUILT-INS
Today many floor plans are built for active families. The plans will show entertainment centers, learning centers, desks, and bookcases. Study the interior elevation detail page of your blueprints. All built-ins will be shown and labeled optional if they are not a standard feature.

CAN YOU FIND SLAB CHANGES?
Using our sample blueprint look for the symbol that looks like a very wide comma. It is drawn with the tail of the comma pointing in the direction of the change in the slab. In the garage you will see a 3 ½ inch drop from the tire stop to the garage floor. Also the entry has a slab change as well as the family room.

Be pro-active. Think of questions buyers may ask and find the answers in the blueprints before meeting with the buyers.

HOW TO SHOW AND SELL FROM A BLUEPRINT

The first time you look at the floor plan of a blueprint, begin by taking in the overall shape of the plan. Is the design square or rectangular? Is the plan a one or two story? Is the plan front entry, front side swing entry, rear, or rear side entry? Is the plan a "C" shape or "U" shape design? A "C" design has a side oriented yard, and in a "U" shape the house resembles a horseshoe.

As you begin to explore the house on paper begin at the entry. Discover the house on paper the same as you would on foot. Examine each room carefully. What are the selling features of each room? Are there any negatives to overcome?

In our sample blueprint, you would point out to prospective buyers the step up to the entry and the step down into the rotunda. This is not just another flat uninteresting one story. If this is a physical tour always let the buyers enter in front of you and leave the front door open. If the weather is cold, rainy, or hot leave the door ajar. Once you enter the house get excited about the ceiling detail of the rotunda. If you are showing this house on paper, describe the graduating ceiling pop-ups. The ceiling moves from 8' to 9', then 10' to eventually an 11' ceiling!

I always suggest that you move people through paper as you would in an actual house. By that I mean always go to the right or move to the left consistently. The idea is to end your physical or paper tour with the most exciting area of the house. You do not want to end with a negative. This will also help you to stay in control and enable you to keep selling and closing all through the tour. Study all your plans and you will discover the best direction for tours.

Look at our sample blueprint. If you enter the house and go to the right, you will have a dining room with interesting ceiling detail. You could also lose the wife at this point if she wandered into the kitchen. However, if you move to the left, you will enter a narrow hallway with one bath and two rather small bedrooms. You will want to get these rooms toured first and move on into the drama of the house.

In this situation, move to the center of the rotunda and point toward the hallway and the two bedrooms; do this both in person and if it is a paper tour. Keep with the idea of touring in one direction. By this I mean if you start the tour moving left in person or on paper, then stay left. This will keep you in control. Next you would move on to the study.

The study in this plan is a real selling feature. Two large 4°5° windows plus a wet bar with sliding mirror doors! Keep left, moving from the study into the family room with the dropped slab floor. I would use the term sunken for more selling sizzle. Looking or pointing left describe the fireplace flanked by two 3°6° windows. Move left along the back wall to share an entire wall of windows! Imagine how sunny, bright, and inviting this room will be all year long.

Continue your tour. Point out the step up into the breakfast and kitchen area from the living room. Emphasize the easy access to the backyard from the breakfast nook. Walk or point left to the breakfast windows and continue into the kitchen. Circle the island and walk back into the breakfast nook. The people will always follow you. On paper, they will follow your hand movements. If this is a physical tour, move back into the breakfast area and let your buyers explore the kitchen. From this point you can easily direct the tour into the master bedroom and bath area.

A safety tip: Always have your prospects walk ahead of you if you are entering a room with only one entrance and exit. After your buyers have entered the bedroom, it is safe for you to enter and stand near the doorway. From this point you can share information and answer questions.

On paper, point out the two wonderful his and hers closets. Discuss the number of shelves, rods, and shoeboxes. If this is a physical tour, never, under any circumstance, enter into a closet ahead of buyers, alone, or with the buyers. Do not go into closets. This is for everyone, whether male or female.

To end the paper or physical tour of this house, walk (or direct on paper), the buyers back through the breakfast room down again into the sunken living room and out to the rotunda. From the rotunda you could direct the buyers attention to the dramatic ceiling detail in the dining room. This would be an excellent way to end with a positive feeling.

On the other hand, if you had begun your tour in a right hand direction the tour would have ended with the two small bedrooms. You never want to end on a negative.

By studying your plans you will learn the best paths to take for successful selling.

ARCHITECT SCALE

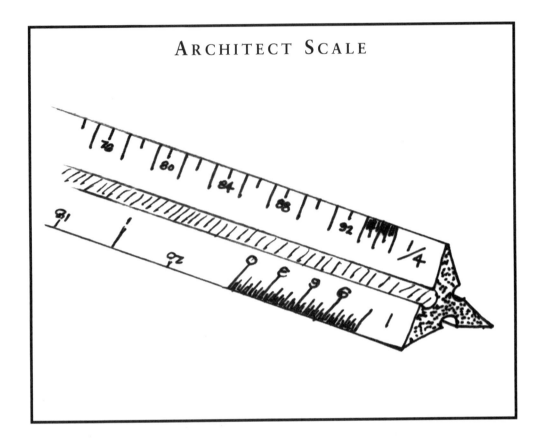

STAIR CASES

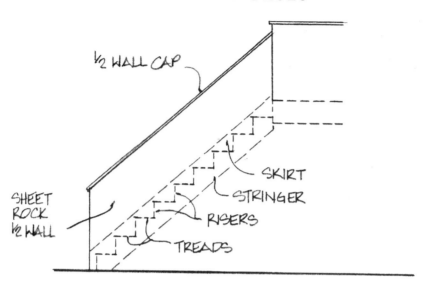

½ WALL CAP

SHEET
ROCK
½ WALL

SKIRT
STRINGER
RISERS
TREADS

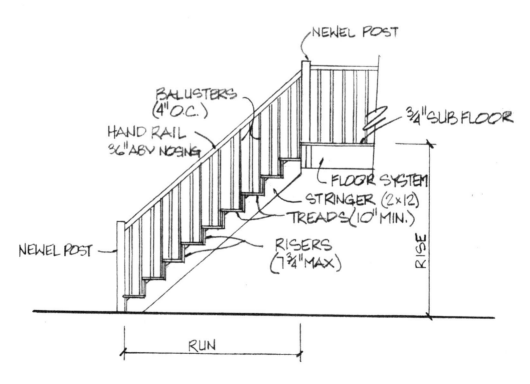

NEWEL POST

BALUSTERS
(4" O.C.)

HAND RAIL
36" ABV NOSING

NEWEL POST

¾" SUB FLOOR

FLOOR SYSTEM
STRINGER (2×12)
TREADS (10" MIN.)

RISERS
(7¾" MAX)

RISE

RUN

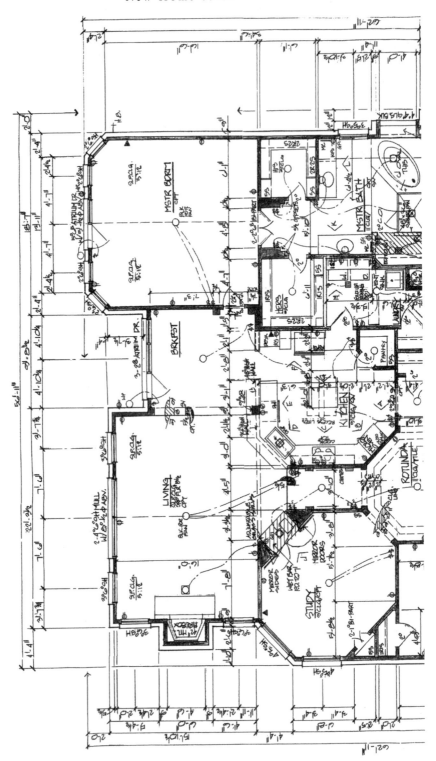

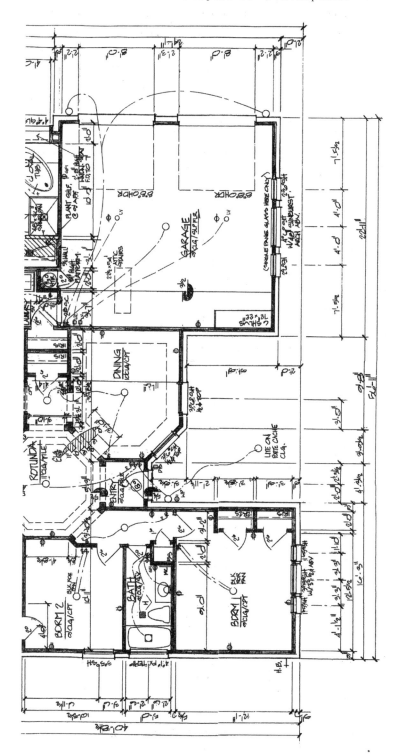

FLOOR PLAN

NOT TO SCALE

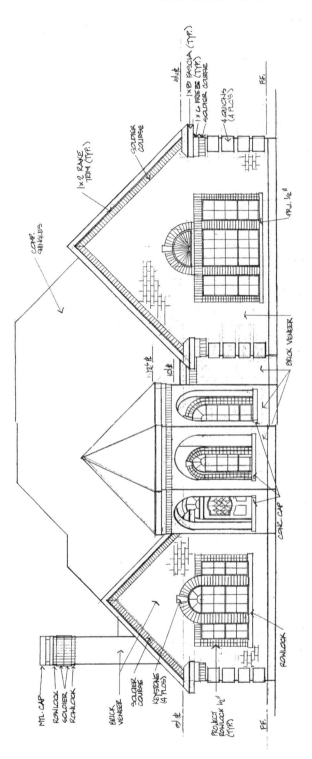

FRONT ELEVATION

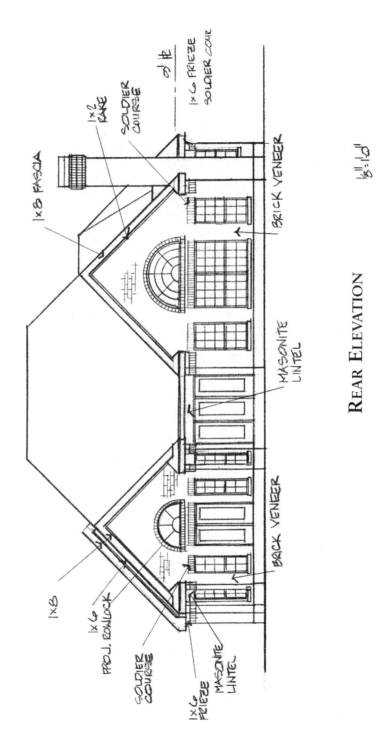

REAR ELEVATION

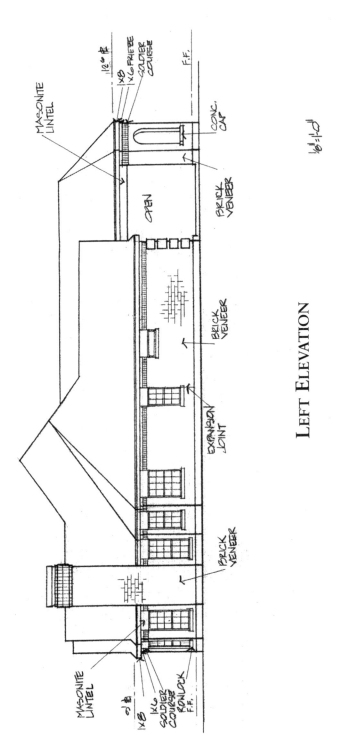

LEFT ELEVATION

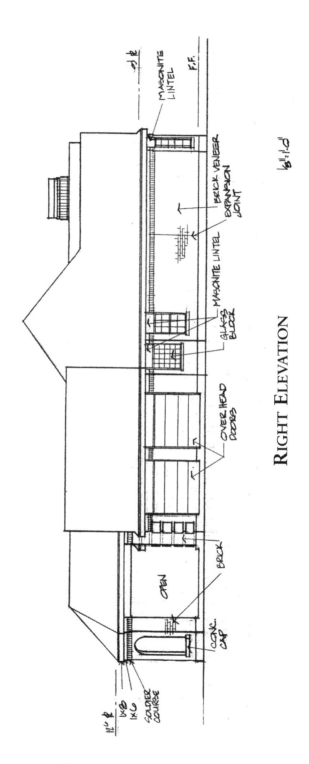

RIGHT ELEVATION

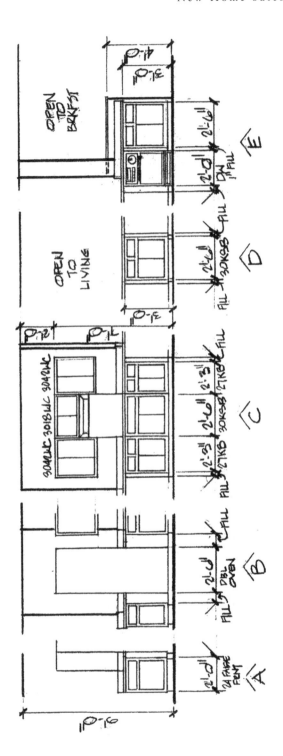

INTERIOR ELEVATION

ELECTRICAL LEGEND

℗	DUPLEX
℗₄	QUADRUPLEX
℗CLG	CEILING DUPLEX
℗FLR	FLOOR DUPLEX
$	SWITCH
$₃	THREE WAY SWITCH
$R	RHEOSTAT SWITCH
$STOP	SWITCH TOP ONLY PLUG
▶	TELEPHONE
▷	TV
⊤	THERMOSTAT
▣	DOORBELL
⊙⊙	CHIMES
O₁	JUNCTION
℗220	220 VOLT OUTLET
⊕	CEILING LIGHT
⊤	WALL MOUNT LIGHT
▢	RECESSED CAN LIGHT
◑	EYEBALL LIGHT
⊙SD	SMOKE DETECTOR
⊜	EXHAUST VENT
⟁	FLOOD LIGHT

CHAPTER 12

PLOT PLANS AND HOME SITES

PLOT PLANS

It is important to know that site and plot plans are drawn to scale just as structures are drawn to scale. The difference is structures are drawn on blueprints and you use an architect scale. Land is drawn on a plot or site plan and you use a scale known as the engineer scale.

USING THE ENGINEER SCALE

On the engineer scale an inch is divided into 10, 20, 30, 40, 50, or 60 equal parts. If there is not a scale number in the top left corner of the plot plan use 1" = 20'.

Every sales office should have a lot fit book with footprint transparencies of each floor plan offered in your community. A lot fit book has an individual page for every lot in your subdivision that your company can sell. The lot drawings are very simple as they show the shape of the lot including the width and depth, along with the building setback lines.

The footprint transparencies are the outline of the foundation of a house. If your company does not provide transparencies you can make your own. Take the width and length dimensions of each house from the blueprints. Most plot plans are drawn to a scale of 1" = 20'. Using an engineer scale draw the footprint. Do not worry about duplicating any insets that appear in the actual footprint of the house.

If the house plan is 52' wide and 70' long, using the 20 side of the scale, draw your footprint. Place the engineer scale with the working edge away from you. Looking down over the scale, mark off the required dimension for the width and then do the same thing for the length. You are creating a very simple rectangle footprint scale version of your house. Handwrite in the center of your footprint the name of the plan and indicate if this is a two or three car garage. Next take your scale drawing and copy it onto transparency paper. Purchase a binder that has several pockets and place a transparency into each pocket or use a 3-ring binder and insert your transparencies into clear page protectors. You will sell more houses when you have tools to help involve the buyers in the buying process.

When potential buyers are showing interest in a specific plan, pull out your lot fit book and begin placing the transparency of that plan on different lots so the buyers can see how the house could be positioned on each lot. Get the prospective buyers involved, hand them the transparency. The prospects will begin to take ownership and start making statements like: "I like this lot better because it faces north, south, east, west," or "We would have enough room for a pool, a garden." Listen for any ownership statement. That is your clue to get the prospects out to see that fantastic lot!

Demonstrating a Home Site

When possible, park your car across the street from the lot you will be viewing. The industry word for viewing a lot is "to site."

Always let the prospects be the first to step from the street onto their prospective new home site. Let them walk all over it. You stay out of the center of the lot. Keep to the side property lines. Try to always place yourself at an angle to the prospective buyers. You will appear far away and the lot will appear larger. Carry your 100-foot construction tape with you. You should always hold the zero end of the tape when working with prospects. Let the prospects quote the distances.

The prospects will be voicing positive and negative opinions about the lot, like thinking out loud. Let them work it out; you have no idea what other people find desirable or undesirable about land. Be quiet unless they ask you a question.

No matter how negative their conversation or body language is about the lot, never suggest seeing another lot while the prospective buyers are looking at the one under their feet.

Let them tell you they absolutely do not like this lot before suggesting another one for them to see. If you get a negative response, do not agree or add your personal negative comments about this piece of land. After the buyers see what other sites are available they may come back to this one! If you get a negative response, be positive and up beat. Smile when you begin to talk about the next lot. Refer to the next lot as a home site and suggest they may find it a more desirable piece of land than this lot. This would be a good time to say "Let's go see some more land choices, then you can make a comparison and decide which home site is best for you." Always leave the door open to come back.

You have now reinforced their opinion that the first lot may not be right for them and it is okay to keep looking. You have also switched the gears in their brains. They aren't just looking at lots. They are on a hunt for their lot. It is no longer about what is wrong with a lot but which is the right one for them. You are there to help them find the right home site.

When you arrive at the next lot, say, "Oh yes, this is nice," then let them start the process all over again. You be quiet. This is a sale in progress. Statistics show 90% of the prospects sited turn into buyers.

Study your site plan ahead of time. You will need to know compass directions. Buyers will ask which way is north. Will the backyard get morning or afternoon sun? Some buyers want to avoid afternoon sun while others enjoy sunsets. If buyers work nights and sleep during the day, the bedroom should not be on the east and rising-sun side of the house. A compass is a good sales tool to keep in your car.

Learning to read a plot plan is second only to reading blueprints. After buyers have selected a plan and a home site they will want to know how the house is going to sit on that lot. This is where your transparencies come back into play. While you are out on the lot with the buyers make notes about the location of gas, phone, or electrical boxes in the front yard if they are purchasing a front entry home or alley if it is a rear entry. The location of any of these items is important information for the buyers when deciding if their driveway is to be on the right or left. These items could also affect their fence. They could decide to fence around the item leaving it in the alley. After identifying the gas, phone, or electrical boxes you should get the buyers back to your office. Simply say, "Lets go read your plot plan and select the best position for your house."

READING A PLOT PLAN

Similar to a blueprint, a plot plan is made up of lines. Each line has a meaning. The lines on a plot plan can be short dashes, long dark thick lines, or x's to indicate the fence line. Plot plans also show building setbacks with short dashes or extension lines. The direction north is always displayed.

Sample Plot Plan: 1216 Star Hill Lane

PROPERTY LINES
Locate the property lines for this particular lot. The dark black broken line indicates the four property lines. The size and shape of the lot plus the width and depth of the lot can be observed.

Locate on your plot plan the black broken line at the top of the page for the width of the backyard. Did you find L = 59'.07"? This means the back property line is 59' and 7" wide. Now find the width of the front of the lot: 62'.67". The right and left side of the lot will have dark black broken lines with the length in feet on either side. The length of our sample is 115' on both sides. We have a lot that is 59'.07" wide in the back and 62'.67" wide in the front with the length of our side property lines being 115'.

UTILITY EASEMENTS
Looking again at the top of the page directly inside the back property line, you will see a lighter broken line indicating a 5' utility easement. Take note that a driveway can be placed over a utility easement but never a solid structure or a swimming pool. Utility easements can also run along the side of the property. If you are not sure review the community site map.

FENCE
The small x's show the location of the standard fence. Our example has the fence on the right side of the driveway running along the back property line, continuing along the right property line then making a left turn to the back right corner of the house. It is imperative that you know the point of beginning and end for your standard fences. You will also need to know if gates are standard and if so how many are included. Fencing material is important. Are the standard fences made of spruce, pine, or cedar? Are the posts metal or wood? What type of wood are the posts? What is the standard height of a fence, six feet or eight feet? Is the top of the fence finished with dog-ears or a cap? Dog-ears resemble a picket fence; a cap is a flat finish along the top. You will also need to know the maximum height allowed for fences in your community.

BUILDING SETBACK LINES
There are four setback lines for a piece of property. These setback lines are also referred to as the building lines. This means the structure must be within all four setback lines. Buyers are most interested in how far their house will be from the front street and how close their neighbor's house will be to their house.

REAR SETBACK LINE

Locate at the top of the page a broken line running horizontally. The rear of the house is on this line. This is the rear setback. (See the notation to the right of this line, 20' rear setback.) Most city codes require 20 feet for the length of a rear driveway. The house is not allowed to cross over this line. The footprint of the house must be within all four setback lines. Let's say we have a much shorter house or a much longer lot and the house did not reach all the way to the rear setback line, you could build a swimming pool over the rear setback line if you have enough space. Only the house cannot cross over this line.

SIDE SETBACK LINES

The second and third setback lines are the two vertical broken lines running from the solid black rear property line to the solid black front property line. In our illustration we have a 7' side setback from the house to the property line.

FRONT SETBACK LINE

The front setback line is a broken line running horizontally across the front of the house and has a notation to the right: 25' Bldg. Line. This means the house must be placed 25' from the front property line. In the same community with both front entry and rear entry home sites, the front setback lines can be different. Study your large site map if you are unsure.

FOOTPRINT OF HOUSE

Within the boundaries of your building lines is the footprint of the house. The width and length of the house will be noted as well as the plan name, the elevation, and the location of the garage. Remember, garage location is determined if you are standing in the front yard looking toward the front of the house. In our example the garage is on the left.

OTHER DETAILS FOUND ON A PLOT PLAN

This is not information you would need to sell a house. This is knowledge to tuck away for the day buyers question all the numbers on the plot plan.

The plot plan will have information for a surveyor to locate this piece of property. Please observe each side of the black property lines on our example. There are numbers listed above or below the numbers showing the length of the lot. These are the coordinates for a surveyor. The numbers read N69°37'54" W; this means north 69 degrees 37 minutes and 54 seconds west and S71°25'34"E; south 71 degrees 25 minutes, 34 seconds east.

You will also see notations at all four corners of the property indicating the existing grade and the finished grade of the lot.

The radius of the front and rear of the lot are usually located next to the width numbers at the top and bottom of the solid black property lines. Our example has an R = 1,886' and R = 2,001'. This gives the radius of the property from some designated point for the surveyor.

On the bottom of the page of a plot plan, you will find the lot and block, community name, city, state, plan or model name, location of garage, abbreviation legend, and the name of the company that prepared the plot plan including the date of the survey. The plot plan will give the linear footage of fence and square footages for concrete and sod.

SOD

The total square footage numbers for sod will be listed in the left hand corner of the plot plan. Some plot plans will have the sod broken down into rear sod area and front sod. This is especially helpful if sod is not standard. You will have the area amounts to give your buyers a cost if they want to include sod with their purchase. To estimate the cost of sod take the area number from your plot plan and divide that number by nine, getting the number of yards in the area. Using your company's cost per yard for sod multiply that number by the number of yards. The final step is to include your company's option mark-up for the final retail cost.

Sod needed to cover the area is calculated as follows: 2,240 square feet sod area ÷ by 9 = 248.89 yards of sod needed. Next multiply the 249 yards by the company's cost per yard for sod. In our example the cost per yard is $4 x 249 = $996. Remember the $996 is your company's cost; you will need to add the mark-up to make a profit. Ask your sales manager what number to use. For our example, we will use a 40% option mark-up. A 40% mark-up of $996 equals $398.40. Add $996 to $398.40 for the cost for sod on this lot. The buyers cost is $1,394.40.

It could be helpful and save you time when working with prospects if you will figure the sod cost for your lots ahead of time and jot the dollar amount next to the sod area on your plot plans.

Think of your plot plans and community site map as treasure maps for you to use to achieve a higher income! Use the maps as sales tools and watch your sales and income explode!

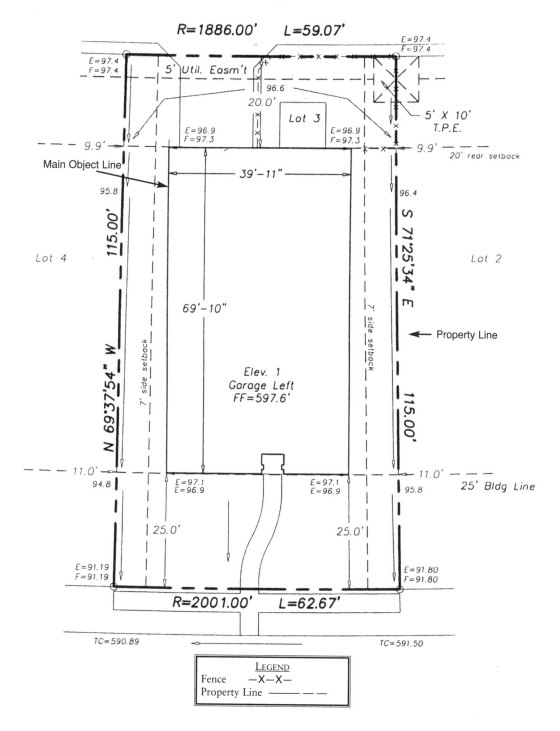

ENGINEER SCALE

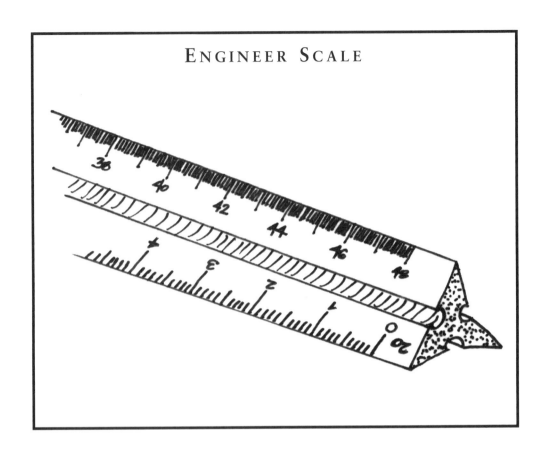

CHAPTER 13

FINANCE

Finance could possibly be the most important chapter for your success. On your first day in a model you could be asked questions like, "How much house can I afford?" Or "How much are the taxes on this house?" If you are unable to pick up a calculator and give the prospect an answer, you may have already lost the sale. The purchase of a house is usually the single largest investment the average person will make in his or her lifetime. Would you want to spend $200,000 or more with a salesperson that was unknowledgeable? Your answer should be no. And the person asking you these questions will also come to a "not buying from that guy" attitude.

Most of the large building companies have computer programs designed with each community's data, plans, prices and options, lots and blocks, a follow-up program, buyer information, finance and loan information, qualifying, and tax benefits. These programs allow you to do many tasks, such as entering your daily traffic, building contact list, competition studies, and generate month-end reports. I strongly urge each of you to learn your builder's computer program and use it!

About now, you are probably thinking, "The builder I work for (or want to work for) has a computer program that does everything for me. I don't need to know anything about finance. I just have to point and click with a mouse and wham! I am there, a financial wizard. Click, print, and I hand the prospective buyers their personalized cost estimation sheet on the home of their dreams. Sign on the dotted line! Next customers please!" If only it were that simple.

Technology is an aid. The computer isn't the smart guy; you are! People want to buy from people. Use the computer to enhance you. The computer was never meant to do the sales job alone. Yes, you can generate a monthly payment cost estimate for potential buyers with just a few clicks of the mouse. You need to be better than that. You need to know more than that. Realize that if all you have to do is point and click to create principal, interest, taxes, and insurance (PITI) for a prospect, your competition is able to do the same thing. What would you do if there was a power failure or your computer crashed?

EXAMPLE:

Mr. and Mrs. Buyer: "How much will our monthly payment be on house plan A?"

Salesperson: "Let's go into my office, and I'll print that information off the computer for you."

Mr. and Mrs. Buyer: "Oh that's okay; we just thought you might know."

Salesperson: "Oh, it will take just a minute. I'll just run into my office and get that information from the computer. I'll be right back."

Salesperson: You return with the printed information about PITI on home plan A. "Here you go," handing the sheet to Mr. & Mrs. Buyer.

Mr. and Mrs. Buyer: "That's great, but this says 10% down. We don't want to put down more than 5%."

Salesperson: "Oh, well wait just one more minute while I go print another cost analysis at 5% down."

As you can see we could take this scenario and run the salesperson back and forth several times. But let's back up and let me share a way to get the buyers into your office.

Mr. and Mrs. Buyer: "How much will our monthly payments be on house plan A?"

Salesperson: "Let's go run some numbers off the printer, and you will have something to take home with you." At this point you automatically begin walking to your office.

Always say printer. Your buyer has been trained mentally to associate computers with completing the purchase process. Example: Go to the grocery store, the computer scans, then you pay. Go to the department store, computer takes price information, and then you pay. Go to salespersons office, computer takes information, then you pay! Remember, for buyers to enter "the sales office," even for point and clicking, represents a degree of commitment on their part.

Now let's go back to the first scenario. The buyers will not go into your office. Every time you walk away from the people standing in front of you, you lose control. And control is closing power. Let us look at you and this same couple, but this time you have knowledge of finance on your side. You become the creator of information. You are confident. Pick up your calculator and run PITI for the buyers then offer to print a sample for them to take home. You are in control; at this point they may follow you into the sales office.

My goal is to give you the real tools you need to be the best. You, as a person, are the best sales tool your company possesses. You, with the ability and knowledge to talk and understand finance, to create monthly payment cost estimates, to compare one loan program to another, to confidently answer questions, must be able to answer by simply picking up a calculator. Never leave your customers. Never give up your control. Use the knowledge you will learn in this book to keep control and build trust and confidence.

I am going to take you through finance in "plain language." We will explore the basics with a beginners attitude. Sometimes training manuals assume the trainee is already at a certain level of understanding. I will assume nothing.

PITI

You have perhaps heard the term PITI. That's what buyers want to know first. How much will this house cost us? What is our PITI?

P = Principal: the amount of a debt minus the interest.

I = Interest: money paid for the use of money.

T = Taxes: a compulsory payment of a percentage of property value. You remember the old adage, nothing in this world is certain but death and taxes.

I = Insurance: called homeowners or hazard insurance; covers fire, hazard, and personal property. The lender will not loan any monies if there is no coverage on the dwelling. If the borrower fails to maintain coverage on the dwelling, the lender may obtain coverage to protect lender's right, and the cost will be at the borrower's expense.

How to Calculate PITI

First you will get P&I or principal and interest. Sometimes salespeople will only quote P&I because without taxes & insurance added the house sounds more affordable. Be honest; always tell your buyers if the dollar figure you are giving them is principal and interest only or the full PITI.

You need only three things. Knowledge of how to read fractions, a calculator, and a monthly factor chart.

Let's start with fractions.

7.000	=	seven percent			
7.125	=	seven and one/eighth	$^1/_8$	=	.125
7.250	=	seven and one quarter	$^1/_4$	=	.250
7.375	=	seven and three eighths	$^3/_8$	=	.375
7.500	=	seven and one half	$^1/_2$	=	.500
7.625	=	seven and five eighths	$^5/_8$	=	.625
7.750	=	seven and three quarter	$^3/_4$	=	.750
7.875	=	seven and seven eights	$^7/_8$	=	.875

Loan Amounts or Loan to Value

Loan amounts are determined by the amount of money buyers are putting down.

Loan to value of 95% means the buyers are putting down 5% of the price or value (100 minus 5 = 95).

```
 5% down =  95% loan amount
10% down =  90% loan amount
15% down =  85% loan amount
20% down =  80% loan amount
```

Example One
Buyers want to purchase a house for $160,000 sales price. They are going to put down 10%, and the current interest rate is 8.375

You have the sales price of $160,000. Now you need the loan amount. To get the loan amount, you need to know how much the buyers want to put down. In our example, the buyers said they have 10%.

$160,000 x 10 percent = $16,000

Your buyers down payment equals $16,000. Now, subtract the down payment from the sales price of $160,000 and you will have your loan amount.

$160,000 sales price
- 16,000 down payment
$144,000 loan amount

You can also get to the loan amount by multiplying the sales price by 90% (10% down equals a 90% loan).

$160,000 sales price
x 90% down payment
$144,000 loan amount

Another way to get the down payment would be to subtract the loan amount ($144,000) from the sales price ($160,000).

$160,000 sales price
- 144,000 loan amount
$ 16,000 down payment

Turn to the factor chart on page 184 and look up 8.375% (eight and three-eighths) and find the factor number for a 30-year mortgage.

8.375 interest rate   7.6007 factor   30 years

To calculate principal and interest, multiply the loan amount times the factor, divide that number by 1,000, and you have the principal and interest.

$144,000 loan payment
x 7.6007 factor
1,094,500.80
÷ 1,000
$1,094.50 P&I

Principal and Interest for a house that costs $160,000 with 10% down payment on a 30-year mortgage with an interest rate of 8.375% equals $1,094.50 per month.

EXAMPLE TWO

Now let's take our same example and do a 95% loan. Your buyers are making a down payment of 5% of the $160,000 sales price will have a 95% loan to value, and the interest rate is 8.375%.

To get loan amount: multiply sales price of $160,000 by 95% = $152,000 loan amount.

$160,000 sales price
x   95%
$152,000 loan amount

Down payment: subtract the loan amount from the sales price.

$160,000
-152,000
$ 8,000 down payment

Or you can multiply the sales price $160,000 by 5% = $8,000 down payment.

Now, use the factor for 8.375 interest rate (7.6007) and multiply the factor times the loan amount of $152,000 = 1,155,306.40 and divide this number by 1,000 to get the P&I $1,155.31.

Now that you can calculate principal and interest, lets include taxes and insurance and give our buyers a truer picture of their costs in a $160,000 house.

Taxes: Taxes are calculated on the SALES PRICE.
What makes up tax rates?
Where do you go to get tax rates for your area?

This is a sample of tax rates for three Texas communities:

City	City Tax	ISD Tax	County Tax	College Dist.	Total
Allen	.5740	1.8929	.25000	.096723	2.813623
Plano	.4685	1.5792	.25000	.096723	2.394423
Frisco	.3727	1.4400	.23504	NA	2.047740

Tax rates are made up of city, independent school district, county, college district, and sometimes municipal utility district taxes.

A good source for comparable tax rates is your local chamber of commerce or the tax office, which is usually located with the city hall or other municipal offices.

Remember: multiply taxes (2.04774) times the sales price, never the loan amount.

Let's take the tax rates for the three Texas communities and apply those rates to our sample $160,000 house.

Remember: multiply sales price by tax rate. Many salespeople make the common mistake of using loan amount.

 A. Our buyers are purchasing a home in Frisco, Texas.
 Sales price $160,000
 Tax rate   2.04774

 Sales price 160,000 x 2.04774% = $3,276.38
 The annual taxes for this property are $3,276.38.
 Divide your annual taxes by 12 to get your monthly tax amount.
 $3,276.38 ÷ 12 = $273.03
 The taxes or the T in PITI equals $273.03.

B. Our buyers are purchasing a home in Plano, Texas.
Sales price $160,000
Tax rate   2.394423

$160,000 sales price x 2.394423 = $3,831.08.
The annual taxes for this property in Plano is $3,831.08.
Next, divide your annual taxes by 12 to get the monthly tax amount.
$3,831.08 ÷ 12 = $319.26
The taxes or the T in PITI equals $319.26.

C. Our buyers are purchasing a home in Allen, Texas.
Sales price $160,000
Tax rate 2.813623

$160,000 sales price x 2.813623 = $4,501.80.
The annual taxes for this property in Allen are $4,501.80.
$4,501.80 ÷ 12 = $375.15
The taxes or the T in PITI equals $375.15.

This is a good time for you to make a comparison of the three suburbs and compare the taxes. If you were selling houses in Allen, Texas, you would probably not use your taxes as a feature for buying in Allen versus Plano or Frisco. However, if you were selling in one of the other two areas and your customers were having a tough time trying to decide which area would be the best or maybe one of the areas has lower beginning sales prices than your community, then this would be an excellent opportunity to let the written facts speak for themselves. Buyers like to see third party information, especially when making decisions that affect their money outflow.

We now have principal, interest, and taxes of the PITI. Let's complete it by tackling (I) Insurance.

Many salespeople get Homeowners Insurance and Private Mortgage Insurance (PMI) confused. The second (I) in PITI is for Homeowners Insurance.

Insurance: insurance amounts are calculated on the loan amount using .006 factor based on a $1,000 deductible.

Let's work with our sample $160,000 house with a 10% down payment of $16,000 or 90% loan amount of $144,000.

$144,000 x .006 = $864
The annual insurance cost equals $864.
Divide the annual cost of $864 by 12 to get the monthly insurance payment.
$864 ÷ 12 = $72
Your monthly insurance payment in the PITI is $72.

Now let's add our calculations together and see the total PITI payment.

$160,000 sales price
90% Loan / 10% down
$16,000 down payment
$144,000 loan amount
8.375 interest rate
30-year conventional loan
7.6007 factor
2.394423 taxes (let's use the Plano tax figure)

Principal and Interest: $144,000 loan amount x 7.6007 factor = 1,094,500.80; now divide this number by 1,000 to get principal and interest $1,094.50

Taxes: remember taxes times sales price.
$160,000 x 2.394423% = $3,831.08

Now take your annual tax rate of $3,831.08 and divide by 12 = $319.26

Insurance: Multiply the loan amount of $144,000 by .006 = $864 annual insurance premium. Now divide your annual premium of $864 by 12 to get your monthly insurance payment:
$864 divided by 12 = $72.

Now let's add our principal and interest, taxes, and insurance together to have our full PITI.

$1,094.50 P&I
$ 319.26 Taxes
$ 72.00 Insurance
$1,485.76 PITI

PRIVATE MORTGAGE INSURANCE

This is insurance issued to protect the lender from financial loss due to default of the borrowers on the mortgage. Think of it this way: if you were loaning me 90% of the money I need to buy a house, you would like to have a policy protecting a percentage of the monies you loaned me. If I only put up 5% or 10% of the cost of the house, the lender's risk is greater; however, if, I put up 20%, the lender's risk is less. That is how PMI works. If the borrowers put up less than 20%, the lender requires PMI.

There are several companies licensed in the United States to issue PMI. Loans that are greater than 80% loan to value must have PMI. Loan to value means the difference between the sales price and the actual loan amount.

Example: Sales price: $200,000; 5% down or 95% loan to value
            Sales price: $200,000; 10% down or 90% loan to value
            Sales price: $200,000; 15% down or 85% loan to value

Remember: Any loan greater than 80% must have PMI.

Private mortgage insurance companies are limited by law as to the percent of the loan they can insure and the amount they can charge.

EXAMPLES:

91% to 95% loan	22% coverage	.0078
86% to 90% loans	17% coverage	.0052
81% to 85% loans	12% coverage	.0028
80% or less loans	No PMI required	n/a

How to Calculate **PMI**

Private mortgage insurance is calculated on the loan amount.

Let's take our first example of the $160,000 house with the 90% loan to value with 10% down. We have a loan to value greater than 80%, therefore we need PMI. The loan amount is $144,000. Using the chart from the previous page select the correct rate and multiply that times the loan amount and divide by 12.

Loan to value of 90% = .0052 x $144,000 = $748.80 annual ÷ 12 = $62.40 PMI monthly.

Now add together your PITI and your PMI for a total payment.

$1,094.50 P&I
$ 319.26 Taxes
$ 72.00 Insurance
$1,485.76 PITI
+   62.40 PMI
$1,548.16 Total monthly payment

Now, let's purchase the same $160,000 house in Plano, Texas, with a 95% loan to value (LTV). Once again we have an LTV greater than 80%, and we are required to have PMI.

Loan to value of 95% on a $160,000 house = $152,000 loan amount.
Tax rate: 2.394423 x $160,000. = $319.26
Insurance: .006 x 152,000 =$76
PMI: .0052 x $152,000 = $65.87
P&I: 8.375 interest rate (factor of 7.6007) $152,000 x factor = $1,155.31

$1,155.31 P&I
319.26 Taxes
76.00 Insurance
65.87 PMI
$1,616.44 Total monthly payment

Short Cut: Here is a fast and quick trick for getting the full payment without having your taxes and insurance figures. This method will give you the total monthly payment within $50 of the actual PITI costs including PMI.

Let's say you are standing with calculator in hand and your customers want to know approximately what their total payment will be on this same $160,000 house with 10% down. First calculate the principal and interest, then take your P&I of $1,094.50 and divide by 70%. You will have a number that will be within $50 of your actual total payment.

$1,094.50 ÷ 70% = $1,563.57   Actual payment - $1,548.16

70% Short cut	$1,563.57
PITI plus PMI	$1,548.16
Difference	$ 15.41

P&I ÷ 70% = approximate total PITI

Be sure to tell your customers this is an approximate total and let them know you are in the ballpark, give or take $50.

Do you want to make a six-figure income? That's easy, if you *prepare* for it daily.

Never begin a workday without knowing the current interest rate. Look up the factor for that rate and memorize it or write it down and keep it in your pocket, or tape the factor on a piece of paper to your calculator. Remember, if you can calculate P&I and use the 70% short cut rule you will never have to leave your customers.

If you are really serious about becoming one of the best and improving your financial sales skills, take the time and do the twelve practice scenarios on the following pages.

After you complete your calculations, do the 70% short cut just for a comparison. (Answers begin on page 219.)

(Work space)

NUMBER ONE

Sales price	$282,000
90% loan	30-year conventional
Interest rate	7.875
Taxes	2.39

Number Two

Sales price	$252,500
80% loan	30-year conventional
Interest rate	8.000
Taxes	2.25

NUMBER THREE

Sales price	$324,000
15% down	30-year conventional
Interest rate	7.625
Taxes	2.38

NUMBER FOUR

Sales price	$168,500
95% loan	30-year conventional
Interest rate	7.000
Taxes	2.22

NUMBER FIVE

Sales price	$275,000
90% loan	30-year conventional
Interest rate	8.500
Taxes	2.25

NUMBER SIX

Sales price	$228,000
80% loan	30-year conventional
Interest rate	7.625
Taxes	2.50

NUMBER SEVEN

Sales price	$146,000
95% loan	30-year conventional
Interest rate	7.750
Taxes	2.25

NUMBER EIGHT

Sales price	$308,000
10% down	30-year conventional
Interest rate	8.000
Taxes	2.25

NUMBER NINE

Sales price	$376,900
10% down	30-year conventional
Interest rate	8.125
Taxes	2.18

NUMBER TEN

Sales price	$176,000
95% loan	30-year conventional
Interest rate	7.000
Taxes	2.35

NUMBER ELEVEN

Sales price	$406,500
80% loan	30-year conventional
Interest rate	8.250
Taxes	2.50

NUMBER TWELVE

Sales price	$100,000
90% loan	30-year conventional
Interest rate	7.375
Taxes	2.25

The best present you could give yourself would be to take each of your floor plans and create a monthly payment cost sheet for each house. Select an average interest rate, run PITI plus PMI (if applicable) and have these sheets available for your customers. On the following page is a sample payment cost sheet.

Monthly Payment Cost

(All estimated calculations based on an 8% interest rate on a 30-year fixed conventional (7.3376 Factor) Taxes = 2.04774; Insurance = .0060 based on a $1,000 deductible Homeowners Association (HOA) $37.50; Private Mortgage Insurance 95% LTV = .0078; 90% LTV = .0052 85% LTV = .0028

PLAN 3142   HILLCREST   BASE PRICE $267,000

5%

5% Down Pmt.	$13,350
95% Loan Amt.	$253,650
P&I	$1,861.18
Taxes	$455.62
Insurance	$126.83
PMI	$164.87
HOA	$37.50
	$2,646

10%

10% Down Pmt.	$26,700
90% Loan Amt.	$240,300
P&I	$1,763.23
Taxes	$455.62
Insurance	$120.15
PMI	$104.13
HOA	$37.50
	$2,480.63

20%

20% Down Pmt.	$53,400
80% Loan Amt.	$213,600
P&I	$1,567.31
Taxes	$455.62
Insurance	$106.80
PMI	$0.00
HOA	$37.50
	$2,167.23

Usually immediately after "How much will my payment be?" comes, "Is there a homeowners association?" Homeowners associations are listed on the closing statement as HOA. An HOA can be very complex. They are in place to protect the buyers' investment.

HOA: HOMEOWNER'S ASSOCIATION

Many subdivisions have a homeowners association for the purpose of maintaining common areas such as landscape medians, perimeter walls, community amenities, pools, and tennis courts—all areas of the community, with the exception of the individual home sites, unless stated in the covenants of the association. There are some communities that have front yard maintenance included in the homeowners' dues. You may hear the term CCR, this means covenants, conditions, and restrictions. In the CCR, you will find all the rules of the association. The HOA sets the guidelines to protect and conserve the appearance of the community. It is usually mandatory to belong to the HOA if the developer for the community has established one. HOA dues are set based on the amenities and the amount of common area to be maintained. Homeowner dues are prorated at the time of closing and are then paid annually.

To keep things simple for yourself, read your CCR and know the answers to the most common questions asked by potential buyers. For example: Can we park our boat/motor home in the backyard? How tall are the fences? My husband drives a truck for XYZ Bread Company. Is it OK to park the truck in the street? Is it OK to have a storage shed in our backyard? What is the money collected used for? Who handles the money?

The best salespeople anticipate questions and have the answers ready ahead of time. They also never "wing it." If they do not know the answer to a question, they tell the customers, "I don't know that but I will find out and get back with you." The keynote here is to always get back to the customers.

Now it is your turn. The customers have asked, "How much will monthly payments run on house plan A?" You provided PITI and PMI information. You've discussed the fact your community has or does not have an HOA. You need to qualify these people. Can they afford this house? Are you spending your time with qualified buyers? Remember the old adage, "Time is money." It's your time, your money. Guard it carefully. In one word, *qualify!*

QUALIFYING RATIOS

To work the math, you have to ask questions. So many salespeople are afraid to ask money questions. Throw that fear out the door. You cannot move forward if you and your buyers do not know if they can afford your community.

How much gross income do Mr. and Mrs. Buyer need to qualify for house plan A?
Answer: PITI ÷ 28%

Use example #1: sales price $282,000, PITI is $2,639.80
$2,639.80 ÷ 28% = $9,427.86 monthly, $113,134.32 annual income

Take the time before you have customers in front of you to know how much income is necessary to buy each of the homes on your builder's price sheet.

The most commonly asked question: How much house can I afford?

Your answer comes in loan amount not sales price. How much loan can they qualify for?

Short Cut: Annual income multiplied by 2.3
Example: Mr. and Mrs. Buyer make $5,000 per month; multiply the $5,000 by 12 to get the annual income, $60,000. Next step is to multiply

$60,000 x 2.3 = $138,000. $138,000 is the qualifying loan amount for a person making $60,000 annually.

Now lets do it backwards. If they qualify for $138,000 what is the sales price? Working from a 5% down, divide your loan amount of $138,000 by 95% = $145,263 is the sales price. How much monthly income does it take to qualify for this beautiful home?

Remember to divide the PITI by your qualifying ratio of 28 for the answer.

Sales Price	$145,263
5% down	7,263
Loan Amount	138,000
8% Interest Rate	
30 Yr. Fixed	
Factor	7.3376
P&I	1012.59
70% shortcut for PITI	$1446.56

Answer: PITI ($1446.56) ÷ 28% = $5,166.27 monthly or $61,995.23 annual income

These figures are correct based on your buyers' income of $60,000. But what if you asked the Buyer a question before giving him the 2.3 answer.

"Mr. and Mrs. Buyer, how much are you putting down?" A simple question, but the answer can greatly affect your commission. Use all the figures above for the buyers' annual income. To get the maximum sales price your buyer can afford, add the maximum loan amount and the amount of down payment.

Try it again:
Mr. Buyer:	"How much house can I afford?"
You:	"How much are you putting down?"
Mrs. Buyer:	"Well, we just sold the old place, and we figure about $70,000."

Their maximum loan amount was $138,000, now add the $70,000 down payment to get the maximum sales price of $208,000.

I cannot stress enough how important the word *ask* is to your financial success. Never prequalify until you have asked all the right questions.

Many times salespeople throw good money out the door because they fail to *ask*. If this customer had visited a community with a price range of $160,000 to $225,000, the salesperson could have missed a good sales opportunity, because he assumed the buyers with an annual income of $60,000 did not qualify for the neighborhood. The salesperson would have given them one of their lovely brochures and sent the buyer on his way, along with their commission. But look what happened when a salesperson asked one question. The "Lookie-Lou" turned into an "A" prospect.

This is why there is more to qualifying someone than just doing the math. However, the math is important, and you need to understand qualifying ratios first and then learn to ask the right questions.

Let's take a minute and talk about the 28% we used in the above math problem. The 28% is called the front-end ratio, which is 28% of the borrowers' monthly income ratio to monthly housing expense. The back-end ratio is a 36% ratio of the borrowers maximum total debt obligations to their monthly income. In simpler terms the back end ratio is the PITI plus the borrowers personal long-term debts. You may have seen 28/36 qualifying ratios. What do they mean? Where did they come from? Well, let's take a small history trip.

After the depression, the housing industry in the United States was almost non-existent. The National Housing Act of 1934 created the FHA (The Federal Housing Administration). The FHA does not make loans; it issues an insurance policy for the lender's protection at the borrowers' expense. The FHA insured mortgages took some risk off the lenders and encouraged lenders to make more loans. Before the FHA, lenders had no standards or guidelines for qualifying people requesting home loans/mortgages. A lender could set different rules for each potential borrower. A lender could refuse to make a loan because of a person's race, religion, sex, and/or marital status.

Fannie Mae (The Federal National Mortgage Association) set the following guidelines for underwriting their loans based on people's income ratio compared to their debts and/or obligations ratio. The maximum housing expense (PITI) was set at 28% of the borrowers' gross monthly income. The total monthly debt was set at 36% of the borrowers' gross monthly income. Soon other lenders starting using the Fannie Mae guidelines, and the FHA would not insure loans that did not conform to the industry standard of 28/36 ratios.

And this brings us back to the 28/36 qualifying ratios.

QUALIFYING RATIOS OF 28/36

Using the Borrowers' gross monthly income (before taxes)
divide PITI by the GMI to arrive at the front-end ratio.

For example: Your potential buyers' gross monthly income is $8,500. They are looking at a property, and the PITI is $2,400.

Take your PITI and divide it by your buyers' GMI to arrive at your front-end ratio.
$2,400 ÷ $8,500 = 0.28   PITI ÷ GMI = front ratio

28% (front-end): Monthly housing expense to income ratio
PITI ÷ 28% = $8,571.43 (As I stated before, work up all the qualifying ratios on each of your builder's plans before meeting the first customer.)

36% (Back-end): Monthly housing expense plus total debts to income ratio

Take your total PITI and *add* the buyers' long-term debts, (car payments, credit card payments, any loans, etc). For our example, our buyers have two car payments of $350 each, four credit card bills with a $50 monthly payment on each, and a school loan of $75. The long-term debt totals $975. Now add the $975 to the PITI.

$2400 + $975 = $3,375 PITI, plus debts divided by GMI = 0.40
Okay, now what? Your buyers have a back-end ratio of 40%, not 36%. How much total debt can they have to qualify and what can they do?

Simple. To calculate the amount of maximum long-term debts take their Gross Monthly Income (GMI) x 36% and then subtract the PITI.

$8,500 (GMI) x 36% = $3,060. Now subtract $2400 PITI = $660 for total debts allowed to qualify.

Your buyers need to reduce their monthly debt load by $315. They could probably do this by paying off one of the four credit cards or by making a larger down payment.

Fannie Mae does allow slightly higher ratios if the lender documents all compensating factors. A compensating factor means circumstances that will offset another. A few of the following would be considered compensating factors: a possible pay increase in the future for the buyers, the buyers have savings and/or a good credit rating, or the buyers are making a large down payment. The list could also include explanations of negative issues on their credit report.

QUALIFYING RATIOS: STANDARD INDUSTRY GUIDELINES

Conventional Loans	90%	LTV	25–33%
Conventional Loans	95%	LTV	28–36%
FHA			29–41%
VA			–41% (no front ratio)

A note here: when using the short-cut of 2.3 times the buyers' income to get the maximum home they can qualify for, this does not take into consideration the debt load of the buyers. Some real estate professionals prefer to use 2.5 rather than 2.3. This will give a higher qualifying loan amount. However, my experience has been to use the lower factor until you have all the facts.

DISCRETIONARY

Discretionary is a term used when a builder is offering a discount for the buyers to purchase in his community. It is an incentive to buy.

Your builder or sales manager, (the person that sets your prices and specials, for this book's purpose we will use sales manager) will have worked any discretionary into the sales price of your community's homes allowing the builder to make his profit and your buyers to have some flexibility in customizing their home. Discretionary is very common in most new home sales markets to the point that some potential buyers will walk in the door asking, "What's your special?" As a rookie, I found this unsettling; it threw me off my planned and quite overly practiced sales pitch. I began to answer these bargain shoppers like an imaginary deaf Granny. "Special, yes, you are right ABC Builders is special. Did you know we have been building homes since 1952?"

EXAMPLES OF DISCRETIONARY

$5,000! This Weekend Only!

Using discretionary to create urgency is an everyday affair, and consumers don't take the bait as rapidly as in the past.

2.5 points discount!
A point is 1%, so in this example you have 2.5 points or 2.5%. Always check with your sales manager, as some managers will allow the 2.5 points to be taken off the final sales price, and others take it off the base price of the house.

EXAMPLE:
Base Price: $242,000 x 2.5% = $6,050
Let's say the customers that purchased this $242,000 house added $55,000 in upgrades. See the difference taking discretionary off the base versus the final sales price will make to your company.
$242,000 plus upgrades of $55,000 = $297,000 x 2.5% = $7,425

Discretionary is the area where most new salespeople really get into trouble.

Ask your sales manager how the buyers can use the discretionary:
Can they take the full amount off the total sales price or just off the base price?
Can it be used for upgrades and options only?
Can they use all or any portion for closing costs?
Can they use it in a combination, like for instance half in options, and half in closing costs?

You need to ask before telling buyers they can reduce the sales price or use it for closing costs when your company *only* allows the discretionary to be used for options/upgrades. Buyers can always remember the statements you make that have a positive monetary outcome for them. Your original statement to the buyers will become a promise from you to them. They will not care that you made a mistake. It is imperative that you understand how the discretionary may be used, and it is even more important that your buyers understand. Always be very clear when discussing the use of money.

You may be asking WHY a builder would care how the buyer uses the discretionary. Think of your options as retail items. You are selling products that your company does not manufacture; therefore, the company must pay a supplier and then sell the items to the home-owner. As in any retail store the retailer (builder in this case) buys wholesale, adds a markup (his profit) and then sells the items to the homeowner.

The last company I worked for had a 45% mark-up on all options and upgrades. Look at an example of $6,050 discretionary; with a 45% mark-up the $6,050 becomes only $3,327.50 actual builder expense. It can be better for a builder's bottom line to offer discretionary in options. A profitable company means greater job security for everyone.

Math: multiply your discretionary ($6,050) x 45%= $2,722.50 (the mark-up), and subtract this figure from the $6,050 to get the actual builder cost of $3,327.50.

Never disclose to your buyers the amount of mark-up your company places on their options and upgrades.

Now that you understand discretionary, let's touch on how you handle telling your buyers about your discretionary figure.

Some salespeople like to tell the customers immediately just how much in discretionary dollars their builder is offering. They think if their competition is giving $5,000 discretionary, the customer should know they are too! I have worked with salespeople that greeted the prospective buyers at the door and almost simultaneously with "Hello," said "We have $5,000 discount!"

My personal opinion is that type of selling is like playing poker with your cards face up.

Some builders reward their sales force when they do not use all of the discretionary by giving the salesperson a percentage of the unused discretionary. For example, your company has $10,000 discretionary and you *negotiate* with your buyers in the sales process and the buyers receive $5,000 of the $10,000 discretionary. The builder rewards the salesperson's negotiating skills by paying 25% of the unused portion.

EXAMPLE:
$10,000 Discretionary
5,000 Buyer portion
$ 5,000 Balance unused discretionary

Here comes the fun part. 25% of $5,000 = $1,250 = YOUR MONEY!

Just imagine if on every sale you made you added $1,250 to your total commission. How long do you think it would take you to get to a six-figure income? Not every builder will reward the sales force this way, and not all builders will pay 25%. These are questions you need to ask when interviewing. You may be trying to decide between two builders and asking these kinds of questions in your interview process may make your decision a lot easier.

Later we will go deeper into negotiating skills.

Another great way to use your discretionary is to buy down the interest rate. This is especially helpful when rates are high or rising. This is also a good way to help potential buyers afford a more expensive home by using their discretionary to buy down the interest rate.

CHAPTER 14

MORTGAGES

A buydown is a type of mortgage. It is a fixed-rate as well as a fixed-term. A fixed-rate means the interest rate remains the same amount over the life of the loan. But in a buydown mortgage we are actually buying down the interest rate for a specified period of time. Then after that specified period of time, the interest rate returns to the original full rate of the note. Many of the lenders that buy or insure mortgages have set the maximum buydown at two percent below the rate on the mortgage note with a 3-year buydown period. Let's make it a little clearer. The buyers need a loan. The current interest rate is 8%. They cannot afford to pay the mortgage at this interest rate nor would they qualify. A buydown mortgage would be perfect for the buyers in two ways:

NUMBER ONE
Lenders normally use the first year's interest rate to qualify the borrowers. If the current rate were 8%, with the buydown, the buyers would be trying to qualify on a 6% interest rate.

NUMBER TWO
By reducing the interest rate the borrower needs less income to qualify.

How Does a Buydown Work and How Do You Calculate It?

The reduction of the interest rate is accomplished with an escrow fund that is established at closing. The lender will receive the full principal and interest payment via the escrow account. The difference between 8% and 6% interest rates has been set aside in this escrow fund. And the borrowers are enjoying making a lower monthly P&I for the specified time.

Let's calculate a 2-1 buydown mortgage. The buyers want to purchase your house plan #3345; sales price of $186,500. Current interest rate is 8%. They have the 5% down payment of $9,325. Their monthly income is $5,500.

$186,500 x 95% = $177,000 loan amount. The factor for a 30-year conventional loan @ 8% is 7.3376. Take your loan amount and multiply it times the factor and divide by 1,000 to get your P&I = $1,299.

Work the math for the 2% buydown the first year and the 1% buydown the second year. This sounds hard but it isn't. Look up your factors for the 6% and 7% interest rates. Take the difference between the 8% P&I payment and the 6% P&I and subtract to get the difference and multiply times 12 for the amount to go into the escrow for the lender. Do the same thing for the 7% rate.

Buydown of 2-1

Current 8% Interest Rate	P&I 1299.	Difference		Escrow Fund
Year One Interest 6%	1061.	$238 x 12	=	$2,856
Year Two Interest 7%	1178.	$121 x 12	=	$1,452 $4,308

Actual cash for the 2-1 buydown equals $4,308.

SHORTCUT

This is also called the fast and dirty method. You can use this for on-the-spot calculating, but a lender will require the actual cash method calculations at closing.

Take the total percent of the buydown and multiply it times the loan amount. On the 2-1 it is 2% the first year and 1% the second year for a total of 3%.

3% x $177,000 = $5,310

(3% times loan amount)

Fast and dirty is always going to be higher.

Let's look at one more benefit of the buydown (the qualifying income).

The 8% rate: $1,299 P&I ÷ 70% = $1,855.71 PITI
Remember PITI ÷ 28% = $6,627.54 qualifying income

At the 6% rate: $1,061 P&I ÷ 70% = $1,515.71 PITI
$1,515.71 ÷ 28% = $5,413.25 qualifying income

The buyers could not have qualified at the current 8% interest rate on their gross monthly income of $5,500.

Since the lender will normally use the first year's interest rate to qualify the borrower at the first year 6% rate the buyers qualify! You have a sale and the buyers have the house they want.

WHAT IS A MORTGAGE AND HOW DOES IT WORK?

What is a mortgage? Simply put it is a legal document that secures the property as collateral.

Most of the United States operates under the lien theory for mortgages. In a lien theory state, the title remains with the borrowers. However, the lender has a lien on the borrowers' property until the mortgage is paid in full. This means if you tried to sell your house without paying off your mortgage, the purchaser would not be able to get clear title. Also, if the borrowers defaulted on the loan, the lender would have to go through foreclosure proceedings against the borrowers to obtain the title.

A small number of states use the title theory. The lender holds the borrowers' title based on conditions. The main condition of course is repayment of the mortgage loan. When the mortgage is paid off, the title reverts to the borrowers.

We have a few states using the intermediate theory, which is a combination of the lien theory and the title theory. This works in that, if the property is used for collateral, the mortgage becomes a lien on the property. Should the borrowers default on the loan, the title goes immediately to the lender and he can foreclose. Once again, it is not the intent of this author to make you a mortgage banker. The hope is to expose you to the most common mortgages and terminology and let you hit the selling street running.

More Mortgage Programs

30-Year Fixed
A 30-year fixed-loan program means the interest rate is FIXED or remains the same throughout the 30-year period or for all of the 360 monthly installments. The most popular fixed-rate loans are the 30-year, and 15-year fixed.

Conventional Loan
Conventional loan is a loan secured by real property and is not insured or guaranteed by a government agency. FHA loans are insured, and VA loans are guaranteed. Therefore the 30-year fixed is referred to as a conventional loan.

Non-Conforming or Jumbo
Non-conforming or Jumbo is referring to loan amount. At the time of this writing, the conventional loan amount was $322,700. Any loan amounts

greater than $322,700 would be called a Jumbo or non-conforming and have a higher interest rate. Each year, the first week in October, Fannie Mae sets a maximum conforming loan amount.

FHA Mortgage

The money to purchase the house comes from a private lender, such as a bank. In making this loan the lender will use the Federal Housing Administration's guidelines for qualifying the borrowers. The Federal Housing Administration will then issue insurance to protect the lender from default by the borrowers. FHA insures 100% of the loan. An FHA loan requires mortgage insurance regardless of the amount of down payment made by the borrower.

VA Loans

The Department of Veterans Affairs (DVA) guarantees VA loans. The DVA guarantees only a portion of the loan. Veterans that served our country on active duty during specified periods may be eligible for a VA loan. One of the advantages of a VA loan is the veteran does not have to make any down payment. Another plus is the qualifying ratios are higher with no front-end ratio requirement and the back-end ratio is 41%.

ARM

This is a loan where the interest rate and monthly payments will change. To protect the borrowers, caps set the amount the interest rate can increase at one time and the maximum rate they will pay. The industry standard is 2/6 Caps. Two percent is the most the interest rate can increase at any given adjustment period. The 6% is the percentage that the interest rate can be adjusted over the life of the loan.

An ARM is a good loan if the borrowers know they are not going to be in their house for a long time. An ARM is also a good loan for borrowers who need a lower payment initially to afford the house. The most common ARMS are 3/1and 5/1.

Let's look at the 3/1 ARM. In easy language, the interest rate is a set amount for the first three years. The first adjustment will occur after three years, and because of the cap, the interest rate cannot increase more than two percentage points at that adjustment period. Subsequent adjustments may occur, once each year, after the first adjustment. The total interest rate increase over the life of the loan will be 6%.

To Summarize
The first adjustment will occur at the end of the three years. The interest rate could go up 2%, and this would increase the monthly payment.

After the first adjustment, the loan rate can be adjusted annually. For instance, at year four the interest rate could go up another 2%.

Let's say your interest rate the first three years was 5%. At the end of the third year your rate was adjusted 2%. Now your interest rate is 7%. The fourth year comes, and you could have another adjustment up to 2%; now your interest rate is 9%.

The fifth year you could have another increase of 2% with an interest rate of 11%. This gives you a total of 6% increase. At this point you have had a 6% rate increase. Based on the 2/6 cap you could not have another rate increase.

Normally, your increases are to bring your loan closer to the current market rate, not to exceed it. The increases could be 1% or 2%; it will depend on the current market rates.

80-10-10
An 80-10-10 is actually two loans. The 80-10-10 is a good way to avoid having PMI. The buyers put down 10%. The first loan is for 80% and is usually a conventional 30-year fixed. The second loan is for 10% and is usually for 15 years with a slightly higher interest rate.

80%: 30-year fixed.
10%: the second loan at higher interest rate, usually for 15 years.
10%: buyers make a 10% down payment.

There are many different loan programs available. Don't get bogged down worrying about learning all the different mortgages. Mortgage brokers are learning new programs everyday. All you need is to have a general idea about the most commonly used mortgage loans. Rely on your company's mortgage department if they have one or use a good loan officer from a reputable company. If you do not understand a finance question, tell the buyers you do not know but will find out. Local banks are a good source for answering mortgage finance questions.

More Terms

Loan Origination Fee
One percent of the loan amount charged by a lender to make the loan.

Good Faith Estimate
An estimate of the monthly PITI.

Escrows
Money that goes into accounts for future payments owed by the borrowers. (Borrowers pay their taxes monthly. However, the lender pays the tax bill annually.)

Earnest Money
An amount of money agreed upon by seller and buyers paid by buyers as a show of good faith that the buyers are serious about purchasing the home. If the buyers decide not to purchase, the seller is entitled to keep all or a portion of the earnest money.

Caps
Borrower safeguards which limit the amount the interest rate on an adjustable rate mortgage may change per year and over the life of the loan.

Closing Costs
Monies paid at time of closing. These may include the loan origination fee, title policy, down payment, attorney fees, courier fees, prepaids, appraisal, credit report, and hazard insurance. Also referred to as Settlement costs.

(Just a note about closing costs: a seller/builder can pay closing costs within limits set by Fannie Mae and Freddie Mac.)

SELLER CONTRIBUTION
LTV above 90% seller contribution 3%.
LTV 90% and below seller contribution 6%.

PREPAID ITEMS
Advance payment of taxes, homeowners insurance, and mortgage insurance; usually two months prepaids are required at closing.

HUD SETTLEMENT STATEMENT
The lender is required to provide the borrowers 24 hours prior to closing a good faith estimate of costs and the HUD booklet explaining all costs to close.

FUNDING
After all documents have been signed the buyers pay money to the seller for the full-agreed purchase price. The money is usually in check form from the mortgage lender.

VOE
Verification of Employment.

VOD
Verification of Deposits.

DVA
The Department of Veterans Affairs, a federal agency whose purpose is to administer the veterans' benefit programs.

VA FUNDING FEE
The DVA (Department of Veterans Affairs) charges a fee to issue a guarantee on loans they guarantee. The veteran can pay cash or finance the funding fee with the loan.

CERTIFICATE OF ELIGIBILITY
A form issued by the Department of Veterans Affairs that establishes the veteran's eligibility and the amount of the guarantee available to the veteran.

VETERAN'S ENTITLEMENT
The amount of loan guarantee available to a veteran by the DVA.

LOCK-IN
A lender's agreement with the borrowers to guarantee an interest rate for a set period, often the borrowers pay money for the guarantee.

RESPA
The Real Estate Settlement Procedures Act (RESPA) is a federal law that allows consumers to review estimated settlement costs. The law requires lenders to furnish the information at time of application or within three days of application.

SEASONED MONIES
Through verification of deposits, (VOD) the lender checks to see if the borrowers' deposited funds have been in the account for a certain period of time.

BASIS POINT
One one-hundredths ($^1/_{100}$) of 1 percent of interest.

MORTGAGEE
The lender of money.

MORTGAGOR
The borrower of money.

Remember, you sell HOUSES not mortgages. Stay focused!

Mortgage Payment Factors

Interest Rate	15 Years	20 Years	30 Years
6.000	8.438568	7.164311	5.995505
6.125	8.506250	7.236610	6.076105
6.250	8.574229	7.309282	6.157172
6.375	8.642504	7.382323	6.238699
6.500	8.711074	7.455731	6.320880
6.625	8.779938	7.529504	6.403110
6.750	8.849095	7.603640	6.485981
6.875	8.918543	7.678136	6.569288
7.000	8.988283	7.752989	6.656025
7.125	9.058312	7.828198	6.737185
7.250	9.128629	7.903760	6.821763
7.375	9.199233	7.979672	6.906751
7.500	9.270124	8.055932	6.992145
7.625	9.341299	8.132537	7.077937
7.750	9.412758	8.209486	7.164122
7.875	9.484499	8.286774	7.250694
8.000	9.556521	8.364401	7.337646
8.125	9.628823	8.442362	7.424972
8.250	9.701404	8.520657	7.512666
8.375	9.774262	8.599281	7.600722
8.500	9.847396	8.678232	7.689135
8.625	9.920804	8.757509	7.777897
8.750	9.994487	8.371070	7.867004
8.875	10.068441	8.917025	7.956449
9.000	10.142666	8.997260	8.046226
9.125	10.217160	9.077808	8.136330
9.250	10.291923	9.158668	8.226754
9.375	10.366952	9.239837	8.317494
9.500	10.442247	9.321312	8.408542
9.625	10.517805	9.403090	8.499894
9.750	10.593627	9.485169	8.591544
9.875	10.669709	9.567545	8.683486

Baker's Dozen

1. Principal & Interest   Loan Amount x Factor ÷ 1000

2. Short cut to PITI   P&I ÷ 70%

3. To get loan amount   Sales price minus down payment

4. Calculating Ratios
   Front-End:
   Total monthly payment (PITI) divided by buyers' Gross Monthly Income (cannot exceed 28%)

   Back-End:
   Total monthly payment (PITI) add buyers' monthly debts and divided by buyers' Gross Monthly Income (cannot exceed 36%)

5. PITI ÷ 28% equals qualifying income

6. How much debt can the buyers have and qualify for this house? To calculate maximum amount of debt take total Gross Monthly Income x 36% and then subtract PITI.

7. Buydown fast & dirty method: 3% x loan amount

8. Total loan payments: P&I x 360

9. Total interest over the life of the loan:
   Take total loan payments (P&I x 360) and subtract original loan amount.

10. How much house can the buyers afford to buy?
    2.2 x annual income

11. To back principal and interest out of PITI: PITI x 70%

12. How much will be needed to close?
     Rough method = 3% x sales price

13. How do buyers calculate owner's title policy?
     Sales price x .00647 then add $1,023 = amount of title policy

CHAPTER 15

FAIR HOUSING

It is crucial to your success that you are aware of federal fair housing laws. If you violate the law you will place yourself and your employer in danger of financial penalties. The penalties range from $10,000 for the first offense to $25,000 for the second and up to $50,000 for more violations. In addition to monetary penalties, if you are a licensed real estate agent or broker your license could be suspended or revoked. You will also bear the burden of the legal fees for yourself and the aggrieved person.

Licensed brokers and licensed salespeople must comply with all fair housing laws. If a real estate license is not a requirement in your state to work as a new home sales consultant, this does not exempt you from following fair housing laws. Fair housing provides equal housing opportunities for everyone. Fair housing is the law!

These laws are to create an unbiased housing market for everyone's protection. If a discriminatory act occurs, the aggrieved person is protected by the fair housing laws and has up to one year after an alleged discriminatory act has occurred to file a complaint with the U.S. Department of Housing and Urban Development (HUD). The aggrieved person has the right to a jury trial. Any act of discrimination filed under the Civil Rights Act of 1866 must be taken to a federal court.

As a salesperson of real estate, if you are unaware of committing an act of discrimination or if you state the discrimination offense was unintentional ignorance, ignorance of the law is no excuse.

A person filing a complaint against you has only to prove that an act of discrimination occurred. They do not have to prove your intent or knowledge of the act.

Equal housing opportunities have been guaranteed for all United States citizens through the enactment of fair housing laws by the federal and state governments. I keep stressing the point that equal housing opportunities have been guaranteed for all United States citizens by the federal government. Fair housing is the law.

The Department of Housing and Urban Development is the federal agency responsible for enforcing fair housing laws. Federal fair housing statutes prohibit housing discrimination based on color, race, national origin, sex, religion, familial status, or handicap.

The Fair Housing Act of 1968 made it unlawful to discriminate on the basis of race, color, religion, or national origin when selling or leasing residential property. Sex was added in 1974 as a protected class. In 1988, an amendment to the Federal Fair Housing Act of 1968 added familial status and handicap to the list.

The federal Fair Housing Act prohibits the following six discriminatory acts:

It Is Against the Law to Discriminate

1. In the sale or rental of housing or residential lots.

2. Through advertisement that restricts the sale or rental of property.

3. In the financing of housing.

4. In the provision of real estate brokerage services.

5. Through the practice referred to as blockbusting. Blockbusting is telling homeowners (for your financial gain) they need to sell or rent because persons of a particular color, religion, race or national origin are moving into their neighborhood.

6. In the appraisal of housing.

HOW TO COMPLY

When you are dealing with prospects and buyers it is important to use the same standard of service. Everyone has the right to expect equal treatment. You as a salesperson are required to work with everyone that comes into your model, treat each customer the same, and provide the same good service.

Once I worked with a new home sales counselor that refused to work with Asian buyers. If a prospect of Asian descent entered the model, she promptly called out to me, "You have a customer." I asked why she would not assist Asians. Her reply was, "Oh, it's not that I don't like them. I just hate how they negotiate you to death."

This is a blatant example of less favorable treatment. A common complaint of discrimination by minority persons is they received less favorable treatment.

You are not allowed to ignore people because of their race. You are always to use your best efforts. Remember, everyone deserves the same standard of service. If you make this statement your golden rule you should not encounter any personal violations of the Fair Housing Act.

But let's take a minute and cover other common discriminatory acts.

A black couple enters your model. Your company recently opened a new neighborhood in a predominantly black area of town. You think they would prefer living in that neighborhood because there are few black families in your neighborhood. This practice of sending people to a particular area based on their race, religion, national origin, color, sex, handicap, or familial status is an example of steering. Perhaps your intention was not to discriminate. But your act was of a discriminatory nature.

As a new home sales consultant, from time to time you may hand-produce a flyer to fax, mail, or deliver to real estate agents or prospects. It is important that the advertisement of your property not include language that indicates a preference or indicates a limitation. For example, you cannot use words that would discriminate against any groups listed in the fair housing "protected" classification. You would not advertise "adult community." This is a discrimination against the protected class familial status. Familial status is defined as one or more individuals under the age of 18 living with a parent or legal guardian. This also includes a person who is pregnant.

Is this discrimination? Your flyer reads "Beautiful community with rolling hills, near St. Mary's Catholic Church, easy access to shopping."

The answer is yes. Advertisements that use landmarks associated with a nationality or religion to reference the location of a property is discrimination. Also you cannot target one group of people over another.

Is this discrimination? In your flyer you used a picture of your sister's two little blue eyed, blonde daughters. They look so cute standing by the community playground.

The answer is yes. If an advertisement has a photo, which implies the people in the photo are residents or customers, then the photo must not exclude any of the protected classes.

Is this advertisement discriminatory? Four bedroom, 2.5 baths, 3-car garage with mother-in-law suite.

The answer is no. It is permissible to provide physical descriptions.

Is this discrimination? Cozy cottage on Lake Louise, 4 bedrooms, 2.5 baths, split level design, rustic paths to lake, sorry, no wheelchairs.

The answer is yes. Reference to a property's location cannot place limitations.

Is this discrimination? Beautiful master bedroom with view of lake, credit check required, no pet community.

The answer is no. HUD has ruled statements that give physical descriptions of a property or conduct required of persons is acceptable.

While working in a community selling homes, it is quite common to become attached to the residents and the community in general. You should never steer prospects to home sites away from customers you think may object to these new people. Or steer people to live near or next to certain people in the community because they are the same race and you think they would have a lot in common.

When prospects come into the model and ask questions such as, "What kind of people have you sold to?" "Are there Asians living here?" "How many blacks have you sold to?" I always reply with a smile, "I don't know." I worked with another salesperson who would answer all their questions with this statement, "Oh, I just sell to lots of nice people just like you." Be careful. If the prospect asking the question is Asian or another minority group, they may interpret your statement to mean you are selling predominantly to minorities.

If you would like to learn more about the fair housing laws you can send inquires to:
    Fair Housing
    Department of Housing and Urban Development
    451 7th Street SW
    Washington, D.C. 20410

If you live in a large city, look in your local telephone book under United States Government—Department of Housing and Urban Development.

Visit the Web site to learn more about Fair Housing Laws: www.hud.gov/

Another important amendment to the federal Fair Housing Act of 1968 occurred in 1972. The 1972 amendment made it mandatory to display the equal housing opportunity poster. Failure to display the poster will be deemed (prima facie) evidence of a discriminatory housing practice. The poster should be prominently displayed in your model home. It is common practice to hang the poster in plain sight in the sales office section of the model home. The equal housing opportunity poster is easily recognized with its black outline of a house with an equal sign in the center of the house.

Complying with fair housing laws is not difficult. Treat everyone fairly and honestly and with respect. Always offer the same good service to everyone and display the fair housing poster.

U.S. Department of Housing and Urban Development

**EQUAL HOUSING
OPPORTUNITY**

We Do Business in Accordance With the Federal Fair Housing Law

(The Fair Housing Amendments Act of 1988)

It is Illegal to Discriminate Against Any Person Because of Race, Color, Religion, Sex, Handicap, Familial Status, or National Origin

---

■ In the sale or rental of housing or residential lots

■ In advertising the sale or rental of housing

■ In the financing of housing

■ In the provision of real estate brokerage services

■ In the appraisal of housing

■ Blockbusting is also illegal

Anyone who feels he or she has been discriminated against may file a complaint of housing discrimination:
    1-800-669-9777 (Toll Free)
    1-800-927-9275 (TDD)

**U.S. Department of Housing and
Urban Development
Assistant Secretary for Fair Housing and
Equal Opportunity
Washington, D.C. 20410**

Previous editions are obsolete

form HUD-928.1A(8-93)

CHAPTER 16

CLOSING THE DEAL

Thousands of books have been written on the subject of negotiating and closing. Many of these books are quite good. Chapter will follow chapter with well-written prose. The authors describe in deep detail the different types of closes, "The Ben Franklin, The Take Away, The Pros and Cons Close," just to name a few. All of these closing techniques are fine if you are an insurance or car salesman. But I found the old closing techniques to be out of step for the new home sales market.

The reason is there are only two groups of people that come out to visit model homes. The first group is made up of potential buyers, while the second group is the non-purchasing "Lookie-Lous."

You could be a world-class expert on every known closing technique, but if you cannot identify in three minutes after meeting a person if that person is a buyer or a "Lookie-Lou" then you should go sell smaller ticket items like cars or insurance.

Purchasing a house is a totally different experience from purchasing health insurance or an automobile. These items are much less expensive to purchase and are easily disposable purchases. A person can cancel their insurance with one company and re-purchase the same coverage with another company with no penalty. Cars too are easy to obtain and discard by leasing or placing an ad to sell. You can lease a car for a short period of time or purchase one. The car is turned in at the end of the lease period and you simply get another one. If you elect to purchase rather than lease, then you have the right to sell your automobile at anytime.

The purchase of a house is more involved. A mortgage must be obtained. A title search and survey are involved just to name a few of the steps necessary to purchase. To sell a house may require you to hire a real estate agent and, depending on the local market, the house could sell in a few days, weeks, or many months.

The homeowner will have a larger monetary investment in a house. Often they would need to sell one house before purchasing another.

The decision to make a non-real-estate purchase could require a pressure closing technique from a savvy salesperson. However, a potential buyer for a house has already used closing techniques on himself to decide if he should or should not purchase. Believe me, few if any prospects will appear at your model doorstep and ask what you sell. People coming to a model home are either lookers or buyers.

If your job is to convert apartment dwellers into homeowners, then you will need to use "convince me to buy techniques." In new home sales, your primary job is to sell houses. Your job is to capture as many of the buying public for your company as possible. You are in the model to make purchasing a house an easy experience for potential buyers. You are there to share information about your company and its product. You are to match buyers with the right house, write a contract and collect a deposit check. You put it all together. You are a deal maker.

Deal makers don't convince, beg, or coerce; they deal! A deal maker recognizes the buyers from the "Lookie-Lous" and then goes about the process of putting a deal together.

Throw out the old ideas of learning closing techniques and negotiating strategies and learn to make things happen. The words "negotiate" and "close" should be synonymous. A person negotiates to reach closure. Closure is a result of negotiation. To close means you negotiated. Closure and negotiation combined equal a deal. Stop thinking about "techniques" and begin teaching yourself to become the beginning, middle, and end of a deal. You have got to start thinking about delivering deals.

The most knowledgeable, most creative, most persuasive salesperson will get the deal because he or she will know what it will take to bring all the parties together. In short, you are the deal maker, and if you are a very good deal maker, people will come into your model and drop several hundred thousand dollars with you, based solely on your expertise in the field of real estate and your ability to deal.

LEARNING TO THINK LIKE A DEAL MAKER

The best deal makers view every prospect as an opportunity to sell a house. If they encounter a "Lookie-Lou," they cut loose quickly and prepare themselves mentally for the soon-to-arrive buyers.

It is your goal to sell qualified buyers a house. That is your only job objective. Each day when you arrive at your model, you should have one thought process, "Who is buying a house from me today? And what kind of deal will it take to get their deposit check?"

Selling houses is about deals between buyers and sellers. The old phrase, "What's in it for me?" is the undercurrent thought in each sale and purchase. Buyers want to get the most for their dollars, and the seller wants to get as many of the buyers dollars as possible. Each party to the sale must feel it was a good deal for them or the sale will not happen. This again is your job to find that place where seller and buyers can mutually agree to accept the deal.

As a new home sales consultant, for you to achieve this mutual agreement, you must have both parties comfortable with you. Both seller and buyers will need to have total confidence in you. They must both feel you worked hard for them. The seller will be happy because you looked after and protected the company's interest. The buyer will be happy because you helped them get the most for their purchasing dollars. How well you handle the balance between the two parties will determine your success as a deal maker. And the most successful deal makers make the most money in new home sales.

HOW TO BECOME A SUCCESSFUL DEAL MAKER

During the dealing process, you must always be in control. The buyers must sense your confidence. At the same time they must feel that you are on their team. While the seller demands your loyalty and will trust you to look after the bottom-line, he must feel confident that you are capable of getting deals.

In short, a deal maker works for both parties. The seller must know that you are working with ready, willing, and able buyers. The seller also needs to know that you are capable of negotiating the best price for the house.

The buyers need to know that the seller is reputable, builds a quality house, and will stand behind the finished product. The buyers also want to purchase at a fair price and feel they got a "good" deal. It will be up to you to create these positive mind-sets for the buyers and the seller. When you do this you will create a positive buying atmosphere.

What is the first thing you need to do to create a buying atmosphere? You must learn everything about the houses your company builds and the products that go into the houses. You need to know the facts about your company's beginning. How long they have been in business, where do they build, are they on the stock exchange?

In the first stages of setting up a deal, you are responsible for selling yourself and your company. Potential buyers are entering into a trust relationship with you, and an extension of you is the company. You and the company are a packaged deal, and if the buyers like what they hear from you about the company and how well you represent the company, their confidence will rise and they will purchase.

You must learn to casually slip details about your company into your early conversations with potential buyers. Without realizing it, buyers will leave your office with an enormous amount of information necessary to make their buying decision.

Next you will need to discover as much information about the potential buyers as possible. Your company will be willing to make a deal with someone who is capable of buying. Your company wants you to deliver qualified, serious buyers. The only way for you to know about the persons' ability to purchase is to ask questions, questions, and more questions.

You need to discover if the buyers have a house to sell. Can the buyers purchase your house without selling their house? Could the buyers afford to lease out their current home and purchase your house? How much cash do the buyers have for closing, for purchasing upgrades and design center options, for the down payment? Where are the buyers getting their money: from an inheritance, 401(k) plan, a savings account, from the sale of their home, or is their money a gift? How soon can the buyers close?

The more questions you learn to ask at the initial meeting with potential buyers, the better deal maker you will become. To put the best deal together you need to have all the facts.

PUTTING DEALS TOGETHER

When you meet prospective buyers the first question to ask yourself is: "What inventory houses do I have that these people could buy?"

If the buyers must sell a house to purchase, then a ready-inventory house would not work for them or for your company.

However, if you have an inventory house at slab stage or early frame stage, these same buyers could purchase your inventory house and still have time to sell their house.

Always try to move your inventory first. It is fast money for you and your company.

Also remember not all buyers who own a home must sell in order to purchase. Ask those money questions to find out what the buyers can do.

If the prospects must sell or do not like the floor plans of your inventory houses, or the time frame is wrong for them, then they are prime candidates for a build job, which is also called a build to suit. Build jobs are your future money.

When selling inventory houses or build jobs, it is imperative that you know all the stages of construction and understand cutoff dates for buyers to make changes. By this I mean you know according to the stage of a house what items buyers are able to add, delete, or change. You will know whether the correct answer to the buyers' question about changes is "yes" or "no." Never use the word "maybe" when discussing possible changes with buyers. Buyers will interpret your "maybe" as a "yes."

It is important for you and your buyers to know that before a house reaches any particular stage, nearly all items for the house have been ordered. All items must be ordered in advance to assure their availability at time of installation. Most items are ordered immediately after the buyers sign off on the blueprints and signoff on the design center options, thus signifying to the builder that, according to the buyers' paperwork, this is how the buyers want their house to be built. The builder then moves forward and begins ordering everything necessary to build the house. The buyers' signatures are usually acquired within fourteen days of signing and acceptance of the original contract to purchase.

Cutoff times can vary from builder to builder, so ask for a copy of your company's cutoff schedule from your sales manager or construction manager. You will find a sample for construction cutoffs in this book.

As a deal maker, knowing cutoff stages will help you put a deal together or know to let it go. For example, the buyers want the seller to install glass block windows in the master bath as a condition for purchasing. The house the buyers are considering is at sheetrock stage. To install the glass block window unit would require ripping out the sheetrock, removing the already installed window, and reframing the wall and headers to support the unit. Also some houses could already be bricked by the sheetrock stage. This means you will have to bring the brick crew back, creating more cost and lost time for your company.

If you wrote this deal and turned it in on the chance the company may take it, you would be setting yourself up for disaster. Your sales manager could decide not to accept the deal due to cost, extra construction time, and delay in closing. This could damage your manager's confidence in you as a deal maker. Sales managers need salespeople who can bring good deals to the table. If the deal is declined, the buyers and Realtor (if the buyers are using a Realtor) could become angry and not purchase anything from you!

If you are in doubt about a change, ask yourself these questions. How much could this change cost the company? Does your company allow this type of change? If it is possible to make the change, are the buyers willing to pay for it? Is there ripping or tear-out involved with this change? Are other parts of the house damaged by this change? For example, if the buyers want to change the kitchen countertops from corian to granite, parts of the backsplash will be damaged in the removal of the corian and require replacement. This means additional cost.

Buyers generally try to get the builder to make changes at no charge to them. You will encounter times when buyers are willing to pay for the change, but your company is not willing to make the change. The change is not possible, but the sale is still available if you are honest and direct about your company's decision.

Builders who concentrate in new home construction are in the building business not the remodeling business.

Ask yourself if the buyers' change request involves a word that starts with the letter "r" like "remove," "replace," "rip-out" or "resurface" these are remodeling terms. And most likely the buyers' change is not a project for your new home sales company. You should recommend to the buyers that they make these remodeling changes after they close.

If you know beforehand the answer to the above questions and you know your companies cutoff time periods, you will be more effective in putting a deal together.

In our earlier example of buyers wanting the glass block windows after the cutoff period, how would a deal maker handle this situation?

The best solution would be to use their dealing skills to make a compromise with the buyers. Sometimes just saying, "No, it is too late for a particular change," could cost you a deal. You need to think why the buyers wanted the change, which in this case was a glass block window. Most people want glass blocks in a bathroom to obscure visibility from the outside into the room.

A deal maker would say, "Mr. and Mrs. Buyer, your house is past the stage for us to change windows. We could, however, include at our cost blinds for the master bath window as part of your purchase." The deal maker has met the requirements expected from the glass blocks; the buyers are satisfied, and the cost to the company is minimal.

To effectively deal, you have always got to be thinking of the reason behind people's change request; you should when possible offer an alternative solution to the denied request.

This will enable you to deliver as many clean deals to your employer as possible. By clean, I mean no major changes!

How Deal Makers "Deal" with the Competition

To put a deal together may involve overcoming a competitor's amenity package, option money, discounts, larger lots, or a better location. The circumstances do not matter; your attitude will make the difference. You will need to train your mind to put aside your competitor's more positive differences and concentrate on putting your deal together. For instance, if your buyers are comparing your inventory house to a competitor's house, and in the competitor's house the buyers will get upgraded light fixtures, upgraded carpet, and money to spend at the competitor's design center, while in your house the buyers will receive fewer amenities and have fewer dollars for the design center, the question is, "How can you get the sale away from the competitor?"

Do you just give up and say "Hey, that is a good deal, you should go buy that house?" Of course not. You should first ask yourself if that is such a good deal, why are the buyers back at your door? Then take a positive attitude and turn it into a selling attitude.

There will always be competition, and you will always be faced with cheaper prices, more options, or better locations. It really does not matter what monetary or material objects the competition has to offer. The most important thing they are missing is you! You are the one thing that can make the difference. You can out think and out sell the competition. Push the competitor's material objects out of your mind. And begin to concentrate on making a deal with the buyers.

Think about all the good things your building company has to offer: great service, quality construction, and, most important, well trained employees. Let the little voice in your head say, "I am here because I believe in my product and I can make this sale!"

Now start selling: Begin by asking the buyers what they like about your house and build your selling position on that information. Put the competition aside in your mind and in your conversation. The less reference you make to the competition, the faster you will get the deal.

When buyers are standing in front of you, don't throw out accolades for the other guy's product. Stay focused and sell yourself and your product.

Real deal makers believe themselves to be the only competition to be reckoned with. You too can become a deal maker!

REGULATORY AGENCIES OF THE UNITED STATES

ALABAMA
Alabama Real Estate Commission
1201 Carmichael Way
Montgomery, Alabama 36106-4350
334-242-5544

ALASKA
Alaska Real Estate Commission
Division of Occupational Licensing
3601 C Street, Suite 722
Anchorage, Alaska 99503
907-269-8106

ARIZONA
Arizona Department of Real Estate
2910 N 44th Street, Suite 100
Phoenix, Arizona 85018
602-468-1414

ARKANSAS
Arkansas Real Estate Commission
612 South Summit Street
Little Rock, Arkansas 72201-4740
501-683-8010

CALIFORNIA
State of California Department of Real Estate
Post Office Box 187000, 2201 Broadway
Sacramento, CA 95818-7000
916-227-0931

COLORADO
Colorado Department of Regulatory Agencies
Division of Real Estate
1900 Grant Street, Suite 600
Denver, Colorado 80203
303-894-2166 or 303-894-2185

CONNECTICUT
Connecticut Department of Consumer Protection
Licensing Services Division
165 Capitol Avenue, Room 110
Hartford, Connecticut 06106
860-713-6150

DELAWARE
Delaware Real Estate Commission
Division of Professional Regulation
861 Silver Lake Blvd., Suite 203
Dover, Delaware 19904
302-744-4500

DISTRICT OF COLUMBIA
District Of Columbia Board of Real Estate
941 North Capitol Street, NE
Washington, DC 20002
202-442-4344 or 1-888-204-6192

FLORIDA
Department of Business & Professional Regulation
1940 North Monroe Street
Tallahassee, Florida 32399-0783
850-487-1395

GEORGIA
Georgia Real Estate Commission
Suite 1000 – International Tower
229 Peachtree Street NE
Atlanta, Georgia 30303-1605
404-656-3916

HAWAII
Hawaii Real Estate Commission
250 South King Street, Room 702
Honolulu, Hawaii 96813
808-586-2643

IDAHO
Idaho Real Estate Commission
Post Office Box 83720
Boise, Idaho 83720-0077
208-334-3285

ILLINOIS
Illinois Office of Banks and Real Estate
500 East Monroe Street
Springfield, Illinois 62701
217-782-3000 or 877-793-3470

INDIANA
Indiana Real Estate Commission
302 W. Washington Street, Room EO34
Indianapolis, Indiana 46204
317-232-2980

IOWA
Iowa Real Estate Commission
1918 SE Hulsizer Avenue
Ankeny, Iowa 50021-3941
515-281-7393 or 515-281-5910

KANSAS
Kansas Real Estate Commission
Three Townsite Plaza, Suite 200, 120 SE 6th Ave.
Topeka, Kansas 66603-3511
785-296-3411

KENTUCKY
Kentucky Real Estate Commission
10200 Linn Station Road, Suite 201
Louisville, Kentucky 40223
502-425-4273 or 888-373-3300

LOUISIANA
Louisiana Real Estate Commission
Post Office Box 14785
Baton Rouge, Louisiana 70898-4785
1-800-821-4529

MAINE
Maine Real Estate Commission
35 State House Station
Augusta, Maine 04333-0035
207-624-8515

MARYLAND
Maryland Real Estate Commission
500 N. Calvert Street, Room 308
Baltimore, Maryland 21202-3651
410-230-6200 or 1-888-218-5925

MASSACHUSETTS
Massachusetts Real Estate Board
239 Causeway Street, Suite 500
Boston, Massachusetts 02114
617-727-2373

MICHIGAN
Michigan Dept. Of Consumer and Industry Services
Bureau of Commercial Services – Board of Real Estate Brokers &
Salespersons
Post Office Box 30243
Lansing Michigan 48909
517-241-9288

MISSISSIPPI
Mississippi Real Estate Commission
Post Office Box 12685
Jackson, Mississippi 39236-2685
601-932-9191

MISSOURI
Missouri Real Estate Commission
Post Office Box 1339
3605 Missouri Blvd.
Jefferson City, MO 65102-1339
573-751-2628

MONTANA
Montana Board of Realty Regulation
Post Office Box 200513
301 South Park
Helena, Montana 59602
406-444-2961

NEBRASKA
Nebraska Real Estate Commission
Post Office Box 94667
Lincoln, Nebraska 68509-4667
402-471-2004

NEVADA
Nevada Department of Business & Industry
Real Estate Division
2501 E. Sahara Ave., Suite 102
Las Vegas, Nevada 89104-4137
702-486-4033

NEW HAMPSHIRE
New Hampshire Real Estate Commission
State House Annex
25Capitol Street, Room 434
Concord, New Hampshire 03301
603-271-2701

NEW JERSEY
New Jersey Real Estate Commission
20 West State Street
Post Office Box 328
Trenton, New Jersey 08625-0328
609-292-8300

NEW MEXICO
New Mexico Real Estate Commission
1650 University Blvd. NE, Suite 490
Albuquerque, New Mexico 87102
505-841-9120 or 800-801-7505

NEW YORK
New York Division of Licensing Services
84 Holland Avenue
Albany, New York 12208-3490
518-474-4429

NORTH CAROLINA
North Carolina Real Estate Commission
Post Office Box 17100
Raleigh, North Carolina 27619-7100
919-875-3700

NORTH DAKOTA
North Dakota Real Estate Commission
314 East Thayer Avenue
Post Office Box 727
Bismarck, North Dakota 58502-0727
701-328-9749

OHIO
Ohio Division of Real Estate & Professional Licensing
77 South High Street, 20th Floor
Columbus, Ohio 43215
614-466-4100

OKLAHOMA
Oklahoma Real Estate Commission
2401 NW 23rd, Suite 18
Oklahoma City, Oklahoma 73107
405-521-3387

OREGON
Oregon Real Estate Agency
1177 Center Street NE
Salem, Oregon 97301-2505
503-378-4170

PENNSYLVANIA
Pennsylvania Real Estate Commission
Post Office Box 2649
Harrisburg, Pennsylvania 17105-2649
717-783-3658

RHODE ISLAND
Rhode Island Department of Business Regulation
233 Richmond Street, Suite 230
Providence, RI 02903
401-222-2255

SOUTH CAROLINA
South Carolina Real Estate Commission
Post Office Box 11847
Columbia, South Carolina 29211
803-896-4400

SOUTH DAKOTA
South Dakota Real Estate Commission
118 W. Capitol
Pierre, South Dakota 57501
605-773-3600

TENNESSEE
Tennessee Real Estate Commission
500 James Robertson Parkway
Davy Crockett Tower, Suite 180
Nashville, Tennessee 37243
615-741-2273

TEXAS
Texas Real Estate Commission
Post Office Box 12188
Austin, Texas 78711-2188
512-465-3900

UTAH
Utah Division of Real Estate
Post Office Box 146711
Salt Lake City, Utah 84114
801-530-6747

VERMONT
Vermont Office of Professional Regulation
Real Estate Commission
81 River Street, Drawer 9
Montpelier, Vermont 05609
802-828-3228

VIRGINIA
Virginia Department of Professional and Occupational Regulation
3600 West Broad Street
Richmond, Virginia 23230
804-367-8500

WASHINGTON
Washington Department of Licensing
Real Estate Program
Post Office Box 9015
Olympia, Washington 98507-9015
360-664-6488

WEST VIRGINIA
West Virginia Real Estate Commission
1033 Quarrier Street, Suite 400
Charleston, West Virginia 25301-2315
304-558-3555

WYOMING
Wyoming Real Estate Commission
2020 Carey Avenue, Suite 100
Cheyenne, Wyoming 82002
307-777-7141

Regulatory Agencies of the Canadian Provinces and Territories

ALBERTA
Alberta Real Estate Council of Alberta
340 – 2424 4th Street SW
Calgary, Alberta, Canada T2S 2T4
Phone: 403-228-2954
Fax: 403-228-3068
E-mail: myroniuk@reca.ab.ca
Web site: www.reca.ab.ca

BRITISH COLUMBIA
Real Estate Council of British Columbia
900 – 750 West Pender Street
Vancouver, British Columbia, Canada V6C 2T8
Phone: 604-683-9664
Fax: 604-660-3170
E-mail: rfawcett@recbc.ca
Web site: www.recbc.ca

MANITOBA
The Manitoba Securities Commission
1110 – 405 Broadway
Winnipeg, Manitoba, Canada R3C 3L6
Phone: 204-945-2558
Fax: 204-948-4627
E-mail: jstorsley@gov.mb.ca
Web site: www.msc.gov.mb.ca

NEW BRUNSWICK
New Brunswick Real Estate Association
358 King Street, Suite 301
Fredericton, New Brunswick, Canada E3B 1E3
Phone: 506-459-8055
Fax: 506-459-8057
E-mail: louisemazerall@nb.aibn.com

NEWFOUNDLAND
Dept. of Government Services & Lands
Box 8700
St. Johns, Newfoundland, Canada A1B 4J6
Phone: 709-729-2717
Fax: 709-729-3205
E-mail: gburke@mail.gov.nf.ca
Web site: www.gov.nf.ca

NORTHWEST TERRITORIES
Consumer Services
 5201 - 50th Avenue NW Tower, Suite 600
Yellowknife, Northwest Territories, Canada X1A 3S9
Phone: 867-873-7512
Fax: 867-873-0152
E-mail: sdean@maca.gov.nt.ca
Web site: www.maca.gov.nt.ca

NOVA SCOTIA
Nova Scotia Real Estate Commission
7 Scarfe Court, Suite 200
Dartmouth, Nova Scotia, Canada B3B 1W4
Phone: 902-468-3511
Fax: 902-468-1016
E-mail: ddixon@nsrec.ns.ca
Web site: www.nsrec.ns.ca

ONTARIO
Real Estate Council of Ontario
3250 Bloor Street West, Suite 600 East Tower
Toronto, Ontario, Canada M8X 2X9
Phone: 416-207-4810
Fax: 416-232-2227
E-mail: tom@reco.on.ca
Web site: www.reco.on.ca

PRINCE EDWARD ISLAND
Superintendent of Real Estate
Box 2000
Charlottetown, Prince Edward Island, Canada C1A 7N8
Phone: 902-368-4561
Fax: 902-368-5283
E-mail:
Web site: www.gov.pe.ca

QUÉBEC
ACAIQ
Association des courtiers et agents immobiliers du Québec
6300 Auteuil, Bureau 300
Brossard, Quebec, Canada J4Z 3P2
Phone: 450-676-4800
Fax: 450-676-4454
E-mail: jpinet@acaiq.com
Web site: www.acaiq.com

SASKATCHEWAN
Saskatchewan Real Estate Commission
231 Robin Crescent
Saskatoon, Saskatchewan, Canada S7L 6M8
Phone: 306-374-5233
Fax: 306-373-5377
E-mail: kbacon@srec.sk.ca
Web site: www.srec.sk.ca

YUKON
Superintendent of Real Estate
Box 2703
Whitehorse, Yukon, Canada Y1A 2C6
Phone: 867-667-5111
Fax: 867-667-3609
E-mail: elsie.bagan@gov.yk.ca
Web site: www.gov.yk.ca

Answers to Finance Problems
in Chapter 13

Number one
Mortgage payment factor for 7.875 interest rate is 7.250694
PMI factor for 90% LTV = .0052
282,000 x 90% = 253,800 Loan amount
253,800 LA x 7.250694 = 1,840,226.14 ÷ 1000 = 1,840.23 = P & I
Sales price x 2.39 = 6,739.80 ÷12 = 561.65 = Taxes
Loan amount x .006 = 1,522.80 ÷12 = 126.90 = Insurance
Loan amount x .0052 = 1,319.76 ÷12 = 109.98 = PMI
PITI = 2,638.76   70% rule = 2,628.90

Number two
Mortgage payment factor for 8.000 interest rate is 7.337646
No PMI needed on 80% LTV
252,500 x 80% = 202,000 Loan amount
202,000 LA x 7.337646 = 1,482,204.49 ÷ 1000 = 1,482.20 = P & I
Sales price x 2.25 = 5,681.25 ÷12 = 473.44 = Taxes
Loan amount x .006 = 1,212 ÷12 = 101 = Insurance
PITI = 2,056.64   70% rule = 2,117.43

NUMBER THREE

Mortgage payment factor for 7.625 interest rate is 7.077937
PMI factor for 85% LTV = .0028
324,000 x 85% = 275,400 Loan amount
275,400 x 7.077937 = 1,949,263.85 ÷1000 = 1,949.26 = P & I
Sales price x 2.38 = 7,711.20 ÷12 = 642.60 = Taxes
Loan amount x .006 = 1,652.40 ÷12 = 137.70 = Insurance
Loan amount x .0028 = 771.12 ÷12 = 64.26 = PMI
PITI = 2,793.82   70% rule = 2,784.66

NUMBER FOUR

Mortgage payment factor for 7.000 interest rate is 6.656025
PMI factor for 95% LTV = .0078
168,500 x 95% = 160,075 Loan amount
160,075 x 6.656025 = 1,065,463.20 ÷1000 = 1,065.46 = P & I
Sales price x 2.22 = 3,740.70 ÷12 = 311.73 = Taxes
Loan amount x .006 = 960.45 ÷12 = 80.04 = Insurance
Loan amount x .0078 = 1,248.59 ÷12 = 104.05 = PMI
PITI = 1,561.28   70% rule = 1,522.09

NUMBER FIVE

Mortgage payment factor for 8.500 interest rate = 7.689135
PMI factor for 90% LTV = .0052
275,000 x 90% = 247,500 Loan amount
247,500 LA x 7.689135 = 1,903,060.91 ÷1000 = 1,903.06 = P & I
Sales price x 2.25 = 6,187.50 ÷12 = 515.63 = Taxes
Loan amount x .006 = 1,485÷12 = 123.75 = Insurance
Loan amount x .0052 = 1,287÷12 = 107.25 = PMI
PITI = 2,649.69   70% rule = 2,718.66

NUMBER SIX

Mortgage payment factor for 7.625 interest rate = 7.077937
No PMI on 80% LTV
228,000 x 80% =182,400 Loan amount
182,400 LA x 7.077937 = 1,291,015.71 ÷1000 = 1,291.02 = P & I
Sales price x 2.50 = 5,700 ÷12 = 475 = Taxes
Loan amount x .006 = 1,094.40 ÷12 = 91.20 = Insurance
PITI = 1,857.22   70% rule = 1,844.31

NUMBER SEVEN

Mortgage payment factor for 7.750 interest rate = 7.164122
PMI factor for 95% LTV = .0078
146,000 x 95% = 138,700 Loan amount
138,700 LA x 7.164122 = 993,663.72 ÷1000 = 993.66 = P & I
Sales price x 2.25 = 3,285 ÷12 = 273.75 = Taxes
Loan amount x .006 = 832.20 ÷12 = 69.35 Insurance
Loan amount x .0078 = 1,081.86 ÷12 = 90.16 = PMI
PITI = 1,426.92   70% rule = 1,419.52

NUMBER EIGHT

Mortgage payment factor for 8.000 interest rate = 7.337646
PMI factor for 90% LTV = .0052
308,000 x 90% = 277,200 Loan amount
277,200 LA x 7.337646 = 2,033,995.47 ÷1000 = 2,034 = P & I
Sales price x 2.25 = 6,930 ÷12 = 577.50 = Taxes
Loan amount x .006 = 1,663.20 ÷12 = 138.60 = Insurance
Loan amount x .0052 = 1,441.44 ÷12 = 120.12 = PMI
PITI = 2,870.22   70% rule = 2,905.71

NUMBER NINE

Mortgage payment factor for 8.125 interest rate = 7.424972
PMI factor for 90% LTV = .0052
376,900 x 90% = 339,210 Loan amount
339,210 LA x 7.424972 = 2,518,624.75 ÷1000 = 2,518.62 = P & I
Sales price x 2.18 = 8,216.42 ÷12 = 684.70 = Taxes
Loan amount x .006 = 2,035.26 ÷12 = 169.61 = Insurance
Loan amount x .0052 = 1,763.89 ÷12 = 146.99 = PMI
PITI = 3,519.92   70% rule = 3,598.03

NUMBER TEN

Mortgage payment factor for 7.000 interest rate = 6.656025
PMI factor for 95% LTV = .0078
176,000 x 95% LTV = 167,200 Loan amount
167,200 LA x 6.656025 = 1,112,887.38 ÷1000 = 1,112.89 = P & I
Sales price x 2.35 = 4,136 ÷12 = 344.67 = Taxes
Loan amount x .006 = 1,003.20 ÷12 = 83.60 = Insurance
Loan amount x .0078 = 1,304.16 ÷12 = 108.68 = PMI
PITI = 1,649.84   70% rule = 1,589.84

NUMBER ELEVEN

Mortgage payment factor for 8.250 interest rate = 7.512666
No PMI on 80% LTV
406,500 x 80% LTV = 325,200 Loan amount
325,200 LA x 7.512666 = 2,443,118.98 ÷1000 = 2,443.12 = P & I
Sales price x 2.50 = 10,162.50 ÷12 = 846.88 = Taxes
Loan amount x .006 = 1,951.20 ÷12 = 162.60 = Insurance
PITI= 3,452.60   70% rule = 3,490.17

Number twelve

Mortgage payment factor for 7.375 interest rate = 6.906751
PMI factor for 90% LTV = .0052
100,000 x 90% LTV = 90,000 Loan amount
90,000 LA x 6.906751 = 621,607.59 ÷1000 =621.61 = P & I
Sales price x 2.25 = 2,250 ÷12 = 187.50 = Taxes
Loan amount x .006 = 540 ÷12 = 45 = Insurance
Loan amount x .0052 = 468 ÷12 = 39 = PMI
PITI = 893.11   70% rule = 888.01

BLUEPRINT ABBREVIATIONS

TERM	ABBREVIATION	TERM	ABBREVIATION
Above Finished Floor	AFF	Interior	INTR
Bedroom	BDRM	Kick Plate	KPL
Beveled	BEV	Lavatory	LAV
Block	BLK	Light	LT
Breakfast	BRKFST	Lintel	LNTL
Brick	BRK	Louver	LVR
Cantilever	CANTIL	Master Bath	MA BA
Carpet	CPT	Medicine Cabinet	MED CAB
Casement	CSMT	Metal	MTL or MET
Ceiling	CLG	Microwave	MICRO / MW
Ceiling Fan	CLG FAN	Med. Density	
		Fiberboard	MDF
Column	COL	Molding	MLDG
Concrete Block	CONC BLK	Obscure Glass	OGL
Centerline	(C) (CL)	Opening	OPNG
Cornice	COR	Overhang	OVHG
Dishwasher	DW	Painted	PTD
Down Spout	DS	Pillar	PLR
Dryer	D	Plastic	PLSTC
Double Hung Window	DHW	Plate	PL
Elevation	EL	Plywood	PLYWD
Exhaust Vent	EXHV	Refrigerator	REF
Face Brick	FB	Sheathing	SHTHG
Finished Floor	FIN FL	Sheet Metal	SM
Finished Grade	FIN GR	Shingle	SHGL
Fireplace	FP	Shutter	SHTR
Floor	FL	Sliding Door	SD
Frame	FR	Soffit	SF

Galvanized	GALV	Splash Block	SB
Galvanized Steel	GALVS	Stairway	STWY
Garage	GAR	Stone	STN
Ground Fault Interrupter	GFI	Telephone	TEL / PH
Glass	GL	Television	TV
Glass Block	GLB	Tempered	TMPD
Grade	GR	Thermal	THRM
Gravel	GVL	Underground	UGND
Ground	GRD	Utility	UTIL
Gypsum Sheathing Board	GSB	Walk in Closet	WIC
Handrail	HNDRL	Weatherproof	WTR PRF
Head	HD	WeatherStripping	WS
Header	HDR	Without	W/O
Hose Bibb	HB	Wood	WD
Insulation	INSUL	Wrought Iron	WI

INDEX

FOR YOUR FRIENDS AND COLLEAGUES!

You can order additional copies of

NEW HOME SALE$

THE HOW-TO BOOK FOR A HIGH INCOME CAREER!

Contact me at

WWW.DIANETAYLORINC.COM

to place your order.